mindfulness
for cynics

aka

CHECK
YOURSELF
BEFORE YOU
WRECK
YOURSELF

written just for you, by
NICK THAWLEY

Mindfulness for Cynics

aka Check Yourself Before You Wreck Yourself

by Nick Thawley

Contents

Introduction

In the modern world, there's one thing that holds the potential for benefits so immeasurable that its failure to be truly embraced by the general public is a real pity.

This thing is the half-toasted sandwich.

Seriously. When you're making your next sandwich, toast one slice of bread and not the other, proceed as usual, and see how that goes for you. I advise taking a seat before your first bite – it's a wild fusion of hard, soft, crunchy and tender that'll not only change the way you look at the humble sandwich, but change the way you look at yourself.

...but that's for my next book. This one is about mindfulness, and is aimed at those of you who have thus far failed to take any steps down what can be a hugely rewarding path because the very thought of becoming an enlightened, at-one-with-the-universe inner-light seeker makes you vomit a little bit inside your mouth.

This low take-up rate is a shame, but unlike with the half-toasted sandwich, it's an understandable one. Those who pick up a mindfulness book to pursue a vague curiosity in the topic are often convinced that *this whole thing was a bad idea* after reading a paragraph or two. Many so-called 'introductions' present the reader with ideas that preach very successfully to the choir, but for the rest of us initiate the entirely involuntary response of a grand roll of the eyes. This is often followed by a swift closing and tossing-out-the-window of said introduction.

That's where Mindfulness for Cynics comes in. With this short beginner's guide, I've done all the hard work on your behalf, stripping out the mystical without losing anything fundamental from what is an entirely logical practice. Finding yourself, discovering Nirvana, and feeling at one with the flowers in your garden aren't the goals of this book – providing the basic tools to gain a deeper insight into the mind is the goal, with the highly convenient side-effect of a happier, more peaceful existence.

This book will introduce you to some simple, practical methods for observing and subsequently taming your mind. We're interested in the goals of the everyman, not those of a Tibetan monk, so enlightenment can wait – for now, let's just take a turn inward, have a look at the mind, and figure out how to use what we discover to our advantage.

First things first

Before we get started, let's get a couple of things out of the way.

Firstly, a little background on your humble author: having been initially discouraged from anything I perceived as 'spiritual' in nature, I have become increasingly aware that it's by no means necessary to descend into new-age mysticism in order to give yourself a head start in the happiness race. I've become a keen student of my own strain of mindfulness (free of association with any one teacher, book, or the compulsion to go barefoot), maintaining a daily meditation practice and previously attending two 10-day retreats held in complete silence to indulge my curiosity. I was entirely sceptical about the idea that sitting on the floor for a little while each day could bring much in the way of noticeable benefits, but it has, so it's not something I'm going to be giving up anytime soon.

Secondly, you should know that this is just a short-ish, simple-ish introduction to mindfulness, followed by a dip of the toe in a couple of pools of interest. It's a result of the secular nature of mindfulness that there is no one book that *captures* it, since everyone has their own take – you're more than likely come out of this book with a personalised party bag containing your own slice of truth cake, with a slightly different icing on it than everybody else's. You'll carve the path out for yourself, practicing on your own terms while picking out ideas from a broad variety of sources. If you pursue that which makes sense to you, and ignore that which doesn't, it's hard to go far wrong.

What's more, in no way do I suggest that the ideas presented here are all my own. Given that the fundamentals date back thousands of years, it would be a bit rich for anyone to claim such a thing (although I've given credit where it's due for direct influences). My service is to introduce you to the core concepts, keep things from getting too serious, and repackage some big ancient blocks of wisdom into bite-size nuggets for easy consumption.

Finally, apologies in advance for the slightly liberal use of the English language that's to come. You'll notice how I *love* to use italics and the 'inverted comma' to help get a point across (if this bothers you, just wait to see how fond I am of brackets).

Mindfulness defined

"Check yourself before you wreck yourself"

Ice Cube

These inspirational words from the 20th century philosopher popularly known as Ice Cube will serve as the subject of this book. Do not doubt the credentials of Mr. Cube – in this particular verse he goes on to assert his wisdom by warning adversaries that 'shotgun bullets are bad for your health', a claim that has been substantiated by literally dozens of scientific studies[1].

By advising us to check ourselves, it's fairly obvious to me that Ice was trying to convey the benefits of becoming more mindful, which can be defined as a way of paying attention, in a deliberate way, to whatever we're experiencing. The way we do this is to practise keeping our attention on the *present moment* – as in, on the things that are actually happening right now.

The activity of the mind is usually so incredibly dominant that our streams of thought carry us away without our consent,

---

[1] The author sadly notes that the rest of Mr Cube's sage advice from this period should not be followed so ardently – in the referenced piece he goes on to 'drop bombs on ya moms' and 'fuck car alarms', highly disturbing behaviours for which professional help should be sought.

and as a result it's pretty difficult to take an objective look at what's going on in there. For this reason, the only way to gain true insight into the mind is to take a step back and watch it in action from a distance, something we often forget is always possible, whatever's happening.

This is what mindfulness helps us to do. By practicing the objective observation of our thoughts, emotions and instinctive reactions instead of letting them dominate, it's possible to start to build a gap between us and them. This provides a far greater level of perspective over what we experience day-to-day, which brings with it a wide range of benefits.

To shed some light on the concept, I'm excited to present to you what I consider my *magnum opus* – an impeccable analogy, custom-built for the modern era. Here goes.

You know when your computer is overloaded with running applications, and performance suffers? When there are a hundred programs running, all doing different things without much in the way of consent on your part, using up your precious processing power for no good reason at all? This is exactly like the mind when we let its contents rule us. We fall victim to the comings and goings of the various processes, with no real choice over what they do, or how long they stick around.

Being mindful is like having *Task Manager* open. You know, the thing that pops up when you hit *Ctrl+Alt+Delete*. We can gradually become aware of the contents of our minds, and when we're *aware* of the thoughts, emotions and reactions that we're experiencing instead of just blindly experiencing them, we gain a far superior perspective.

As any techie will tell you, we can get a load of useful info from such a perspective – in our case, noticing which thoughts tend to surface the most, or which ones tend to bring up certain emotions, for example. Pay close attention and we can even find some things we had no idea were there – long-hidden complexes or desires like viruses, Trojan horses, or whatever the hacker kids are using these days.

Don't worry if the concept isn't crystal clear at this stage – trying to understand mindfulness by reading its definition is like trying to learn how to swim by reading a swimming textbook. It's far more important to get out there/in there and experience it for yourself, and fortunately, mindfulness can be practised in a number of easy ways (*meditation* being the most common). Once you've read over the basic ideas and start putting them into practice, the proof will become evident in the pudding of life.

Stick around and we'll go through the easiest, most convenient, and most effective techniques – but first, let's set the scene a little.

So hot right now

I'm guessing that part of the reason that you picked up this book is that the *m-word* has started to make appearances in your life that have become so regular that you had to do something about it.

As I'm sure you've noticed, mindfulness is *everywhere* these days. You can't leave your front door without talking to someone whose health club has just started to offer classes. Prisons worldwide are offering meditation courses to inmates, with the US Army and Navy SEALs using it to reduce battle stress[i]. Companies all over the world are offering mindfulness classes to their employees in the name of productivity, with Silicon Valley starting to see it as a sort of 'software upgrade' for the brain: Facebook and Twitter have reported that they're doing 'all they can to stay ahead in the mindfulness race'[ii], and Google has gone so far as to build 'labyrinths' for employees to lose themselves in walking meditation.

Mindfulness programmes have also exploded in classrooms, and Schools Minister David Laws said in March 2014 regarding adding it to the curriculum that "we certainly think that it is an area that merits consideration based on the evidence we've seen to date"[iii]. Who knows, give it a couple of years and your kids could be meditating at school to keep them switched on after lunch.

It may seem like a fad, the next 'oh look at this so-very-new-age thing that I do now, have you not heard about it, *where have you been*?' kind of deal. And for many people it will be just that – something they dabble with while its *en vogue* (just to keep up with the Joneses, who apparently meditate face-to-face as a couple twice a day). However, consider for a second if, for the increasing number of people who have dabbled and actually found it effective, it *wasn't* just a fad. What if the *m-word* we keep hearing isn't going anywhere anytime soon?

In fact, the scientific community is working overtime to find out whether there's actually any point to the whole thing, since there's quite a lot of catching up to do: pretty much every piece of research before the millennium is now regarded as unreliable, thanks to pathetically low experimental standards. It's hardly surprising that some of the biggest benefits of meditation were found by the Transcendental Meditation institute, an organisation worth over $3 billion worldwide that charges thousands of dollars to teach you their technique – it's like Marlboro announcing they've done a bit of research in their car park with two employees and found that their cigarettes *aren't actually that bad.*

However, experimental standards have gotten a lot tighter, and the findings from the last decade have been very promising. To summarise the last 10 years' worth of research: it looks like mindfulness and meditation could be the bees' knees, but it's probably a little early to be making any big conclusions. Recent studies have shown links between mindfulness practice and the improvement of things like concentration, problem-solving and emotional regulation[iv], as well as the reduction of anxiety, pain, and depression[v]. Research using advances in neuroimaging have shown that meditation actually *works out* the grey matter in certain parts of the brain and makes it bigger – an effect displayed in the areas associated with learning, memory and compassion, amongst others[vi]. Things are getting truly sci-fi now – it's looking like we can beef up our brains on a meditation cushion just like we'd hone our bodies at the gym. Nice.

One of the most promising findings is that mindfulness meditation reduces secretion of the stress hormone, cortisol[vii]. Decades of research into the effects of releasing too much cortisol has shown that it can lead to depression, dementia, diabetes, cancer, and most commonly, heart disease, so if mindfulness could help to reduce excess cortisol levels, the potential implications are massive.

Don't get me wrong, the research isn't quite substantial enough yet to make any specific conclusions – *meditation reduces heart disease* would definitely be a stretch at this stage. However, when numerous studies conducted in good scientific conditions start to show that a free, simple and accessible technique such as mindfulness meditation could (potentially) have such wide-ranging psychological and physiological benefits, it's (potentially) time to start paying attention.

Myth busting

Pretty much all mindfulness literature starts off by busting some big ugly myths in the first section. Unfortunately, at the time of writing this is still essential, due to the existence of widespread misconceptions that consistently overshadow the basic fundamentals of the technique.

MYTH #1: *Don't you have to be an airy-fairy tree-hugging soul-searching hippie to be into this stuff? I'm a person of the real world, of practical common sense, and I'm not going to delude myself with this nonsense.*

Although the key ideas date back thousands of years and have Buddhist origins, the concept of mindfulness is completely congruent with rationality, scientific thought, and simple common sense. The student body is made up by gurus, monks, and Zen masters, but also increasingly by bankers, teachers, artists, and athletes – basically, anyone who's interested in how having a look at the mind can help us have a better time of it all.

The conclusions you'll reach aren't taken from any one teacher or book – they're arrived at gradually, with your own personal experience being the main source of learning. For this reason, it's not a case of deciding whether or not you 'believe' in anything or not. Practicing mindfulness is more like keeping up something that you've come to know is good for you, like eating well, or flossing your teeth.

MYTH #2: *I have no interest in escaping reality to float off into cloud-cuckoo-land. There are things to do and people to see.*

By cultivating mindfulness you're actually tightening your grip on reality – learning to look it square in the eye, rather than forever wishing it was different in some way as we often do. Starting up a practice does not require you to move to the Himalayas and abstain from sin, sex, food, fun, and Netflix – it's completely compatible with a busy schedule, and can actually bring the biggest benefits in this case. You don't need to spend two hours a day in meditation to practise mindfulness – in fact, you can get started without meditating at all if you really don't want to.

MYTH #3: *I've heard that mindfulness can make me more content with what I've got. Isn't this at odds with achievement? If I am always content, I lose the incentive to work hard to improve my life, and I'll never reach my potential.*

Cultivate mindfulness and you'll reduce your reliance on perfect circumstances to feel content, but this doesn't mean you'll lose the incentive to do the best you can anyway. In fact, your ambitions for achievement can grow the more that the outcome of your efforts no longer absolutely determines your state of mind. For example, when the prospect of failure no longer threatens to flatten your self-esteem, it's easier to build up the courage to break the mould and set your sights higher.

When you stop defining yourself entirely by the fruits of your labour – which are half chance anyway – life will cease to feel like a heavy burden on your back, and the more fun you'll be able to have in going for your goals.

MYTH #4: *I already have a full-time job, go to the gym, and have to pick up the kids from school. Sorry, but I'm way too busy to add another time commitment to my schedule.*

It does not take a sizeable amount of time or effort to get started – I'm going to show you techniques that can be practised wherever you are, whatever you're doing: during your commute, in line at the post office, or while eating your dinner. This book isn't going to try to rearrange your life – the purpose is to show you how you can take those first little itsy-bitsy teeny-weeny steps to a happier, more mindful existence.

My goal is to provide just enough theory for you to try mindfulness for yourself to get a taste of the benefits. In other words, I'm going to give you a slice of mindfulness pie so thin that you can't help but digest it, and once you have, you'll be hungry for more.

What's in it for you?

Mindfulness is, basically, really, really, really, good. The rest of the book will discuss the ins and outs of why in greater depth, but for your convenience, I'll quickly go over the main benefits:

1) True insight into the reality of the mind

Interest in a path like mindfulness stems from the vague curiosity that there are some deeper truths into the way the mind works that we're probably better off knowing. In fact, the operation of the mind is something with incredible amounts of untapped potential with regards to improving our day-to-day existence. This is because what we encounter on the outside is not important in an absolute sense – far more important is how it's interpreted by the mind, which almost exclusively determines the quality of our experience.

It's therefore common sense to take an objective look at the mind and see if it's operating in the best way – something that we often don't realise is entirely within our control. By taking our attention to the root of our experience, we can observe the realities of the mind for ourselves, and use what we learn to have a better time of it all.

2) Peace of mind all the time, not just when things are going well

We often have a tendency to get so emotionally involved with the current circumstances of our lives that we can lose perspective, forgetting that ups and downs are as inevitable as changes in the weather. By cultivating mindfulness, it becomes easier to navigate through the twists and turns of life with peace of mind intact.

The practice of mindfulness stems from the understanding that there are some things in life that we can't change, and some things that we can, and choosing to focus on the latter. Although we often can't affect what's going on outside of ourselves, we can take the power back by learning to control our *response* to what happens. This way, when life brings us bad breaks and setbacks, we're empowered to decide whether we enter into a spiral of unhelpful negativity, or whether we dust ourselves off and take a practical look at how to move forward.

3) Reduce of the impact of habitual negativity

Going through life operating on the mind's default settings inevitably leads to discontent and suffering. It's in our wiring to always looking for what's wrong, even though in reality, everything's usually pretty alright – resulting in discontent, stress, frustration, insecurity, jealousy and the rest – a whole lot of entirely unnecessary negativity that only serves to make existence feel like a bit of a drag sometimes. However, just as with any other body part, it's well within in our power to change our minds.

The simple act of keeping a mindful eye on what's going on in the mind helps us to become familiar with our instinctive negative reactions and the deep-rooted mechanisms that cause them, such as the habit of habitually craving what we've perceive as 'good', and resisting the 'bad'. The more clued-up we are on how these mechanisms operate, the easier it will be to prevent negative emotions from dominating us.

Of course, this is not to say that negative emotions are unhealthy. Feeling down some of the time is completely natural, and no one's saying we should try and eradicate this. Instead, mindfulness trains us to allow whatever emotions want to rise up, rise up, and helps us to look at them a little more objectively. When we gain this improved perspective over our emotions, we relieve them of the power to shake us right down to the core.

4) A well-oiled, efficient instrument for a working mind, with positive effects on focus, problem solving and creativity

The mind is a very productive and very useful tool, but it would be a more productive and more useful tool if we could learn to *give it a rest* sometimes. Habitually hyperactive, the mind is always looking for solutions to problems that we don't even need solving, since it's in our wiring to find some to-dos to-do when all the previous to-dos are to-done. Without taming this non-stop activity, it can be difficult to utilise the mind in the most efficient way.

Cultivating mindfulness is the equivalent to finally locating the standby button on a traction engine that's not far off from exploding, and pressing it whenever we've consciously decided there's no problem that needs solving for the time being. Then, when we do decide that we want to enlist its help, we're greeted by a well-rested mind that's free to work on the problems we've given it in peace, uncovering a mental environment far more conducive to coming up with effective solutions.

5) Getting more in tune with your likes, dislikes, talents, and desires

In general, we go through life slowly and vaguely becoming aware of our unique bundle of talents and sensitivities – how we're inherently different from the next person. Mindful self-observation fast-tracks this process by raising our awareness of what floats our boats, making it easier to make decisions, both short and long-term, that are suited to us. Clearing away the cobwebs in the mind allows us to get in touch with our natural sense of intuition, which can provide valuable insight into the big questions – should I ask my boss for a transfer? Do I really love my husband? Do I want Popcorn Chicken or a Big Daddy box meal?

Here we go, here we go, here we go

Lucky for you, everything listed above is right there on a plate – a plate well within reach of where you're sitting now.

The tricky thing for me is that these will just appear like false promises until you actually try it out and see for yourself – each bit of learning is done on the level of personal experience rather than intellect, so you won't get anything by watching from the sidelines.

So read the instructions, get out into the world, and give it a whirl. No leaps of faith required – just monitor your own experience, see how you go, and draw your own conclusions from there.

Part 1: How To Check Yourself

This section is the juicy part – where we'll learn exactly how to massage some mindfulness into the tense shoulders of our lives.

This section will cover:

> The difference between thinking and awareness, and why chumming up with the latter is highly worthwhile

> The characteristics of the present moment, and why occasionally sticking our attention there is *extremely* worthwhile

> A deeper look at what mindfulness is, with handy practical instructions to take your understanding to the level of undeniable experience

Let's get started by seeing how being swept away by the activity of our minds isn't actually the only way to spend our time. Although it may not seem that way, we actually have a whole other mode of operation at our disposal.

Awareness vs thought

At the root of the practice of mindfulness is maintaining a state of *awareness*. Although awareness and thinking both stem from activity up there in the wrinkly pink, they are very, very different states of mind.

Being in a state of awareness differs from thinking in that there is no narration from the little voice inside our heads. It's being attentive to the *raw data* of our experience, right at this very second, without doing anything in particular with that information.

Awareness is putting your attention on:

> The feeling of your hands on this book

> The temperature in the room

> The feeling of your bum on the chair

Try keeping keep your attention on one of the above for 30 seconds. Notice how it's not necessary for thought to be present in order to just be *aware* of things that you experience.

In contrast, the thinking mind goes one step further, and habitually takes this raw data and labels it, judges it, and turns it into a thought (or more commonly, a big stream of thoughts):

> It's a little cold this morning. Why am I cold? In fact, I'm really cold! Oh god, I've got the flu again, haven't I! Typical.

Wait, aren't you hot if you've got the flu? Better call in sick just in case.

> This kindle cover is really nice and soft. It's like I'm stroking a baby's hair while I'm reading, wow. I should cover all of my possessions in this material. What's it called anyway? It's kinda velvety. Or is it silky? Or is it a mix? Can they do that?

> This chair is not very comfy. Maybe I should go read in bed. Maybe I should just *go* to bed. Hmm, it's only 5pm, can I really call it a day already? Alright, alright, I'll wait til 6.

The activity of the thinking mind can be imagined as a raging waterfall. Thoughts, emotions, reactions, judgements and desires whizz past constantly without our consent, and we spend most of our time with our heads dunked inside this waterfall. It's no wonder that we don't have a great deal of perspective over what we experience.

Awareness is akin to stepping onto a secret little ledge behind the waterfall, and watching it rage on from a distance. This creates a gap between the observer and the observed: rather than being angry, for example, we can start to be *aware* of the anger. Rather than desperately craving a chocolate bar, we can have a look at *what it's like* to be desperately craving a chocolate bar.

Since awareness happens first, there is literally no facet of our experience that can't be observed in this way. The waterfall rages on, different each moment, but we'll always be able to step back onto the same ledge.

As we'll find out, there are lots and lots and lots of advantages to getting familiar with this vantage point. Let's not carried away though: first let's find out how to get there.

There's a party in the present, and everyone's invited

It's time to invite you into awareness' home. Where it likes to kick back, and observe. Welcome, ladies and gentlemen, to the present.

It can be easy to think that the philosophy of 'living in the present' suggests that you should spontaneously re-mortgage your house in order to buy a 40ft yacht, because, you know, live for the present, yeah! *It does not suggest this.*

Rather than prioritising current events over future ones, living in the present is about being mentally engaged with what's really and indisputably happening *right now*, rather than with things that did happen, didn't happen, might happen, or might not happen.

When you think about it, the present is the only tense that even exists. 'Past' and 'future' only exist as memories and projections – when we remember the past, we're doing it now, and when we wonder about the future, we're also doing it now. Similarly, when that thing that happened to us a week ago happened to us, it was the present moment while it was happening, and when that thing that's going to happen to us in a week's time happens to us, it will be the present moment when it happens. Simply put: it's always now.

Regardless, we spend an awful lot of time mentally 'time travelling' far away from the present, into the future or the past. Although this can be useful in a practical sense, losing the present often serves to cause us suffering.

For example, we tend to conjure up and worry about countless potential future situations that likely won't even exist, instead of focusing on the reality of what we can do with what's actually happening now. If we're not fretting, we're daydreaming about reaching some set of future circumstances that would be superior to the current ones – if only I had this, that, him, or her, *then* I'd be happy.

In regard to the past, we habitually replay it in our heads like a mental highlight reel, resisting the actuality of our present situation by obsessing about what happened yesterday, what we *wish* had happened, and how we *wish* things had turned out. What's more, we often spend ages feeling guilt and regret over what we should have done, would have done, or could have done.

However, as revolutionary philosopher Beverley Knight quite rightly told us, shoulda woulda coulda means we're outta time. The past and future don't exist, ever, so the more time we're mentally engaged with them, the less we're cementing ourselves in reality. This doesn't suggest that we shouldn't learn from the past, or plan for the future: it just means that since our lives are solely made up of a succession of present moments, the quality of that life will be largely dependent on our relationship with the present itself.

Deliberate techniques like the ones I'll describe are not the only way to get to the present, and in fact, you're probably there more often than you think. When you reflect on the times you've spent there, you'll realise that it's pretty cool. It's where you are when:

> you're in the midst of an extremely competitive tournament-deciding game of ping pong on holiday
> you're listening, entranced, to every beat and gradual development in your favourite house tune
> you reach the lookout on a massive hill after a three hour hike, and the view leaves you completely speechless

When we're engaged with *right now*, there's no opportunity for thought to barge in and impose itself on what we're experiencing – life is just happening, undiluted, with no mental narrative. Usually, the mind will come in and label our experiences after the fact, but when we're engaged with nothing but the present, it's a great place to be. This is why activities that we're really into – doing a bit of knitting, tending to the garden, playing a musical instrument, perhaps

– can be so therapeutic. Our joy comes out of being rooted in the present, fully engaged with the *doing* itself.

To illustrate, think back to 1974, to Davey Gilmour on stage with Pink Floyd. When it was his time to shine on, you crazy diamond, he wasn't *thinking* about the finger-logistics of his kick-ass solo. It was just flowing out of his fingers from within. He wasn't rapidly producing thoughts about what note to play next, how long to sustain said note, or looking ahead to what particular cocktail of fun chemicals he was going to opt for after the show. The inner state apart from thought was expressing itself through his fingers, without the usual middle man, in the form of tasty, succulent licks that could feed a family for days. Gilmour was fretting without fretting, and all that was left was the undiluted experience of the moment – the reason that his face-scrunching solos ended up so enjoyable for everybody involved, especially him.

Conveniently, there's an easy way to deliberately strengthen our relationship with the present and get into this state whenever we fancy it – and I'm sure that by now, you've managed to guess what it is.

So we've finally reached the mindfulness section in a book about mindfulness! If you haven't been, it's probably time for you to start *paying attention*. Heh.

Although you two met earlier, I'll briefly reintroduce you to avoid any potential embarrassment. Mindfulness is the practice of staying actively engaged with the present moment, in order to become aware of everything that's happening there – sensations we sense, thoughts we think, emotions we.. emote. There's a difference between mindfulness and simply being engaged with the present moment: mindfulness involves keeping our attention there *on purpose*.

To illustrate: Dave Gilmour may well have been fully engaged with the present moment during his solo, but it's unlikely that he was practicing mindfulness. A mindful Gilmour would have been paying *deliberate* attention to everything that he was experiencing: the noise of the crowd, the heat from the lights, and the sweat dripping down his forehead. While you can end up engaged with the present by chance, practicing mindfulness requires a targeted effort. If the difference between the two isn't entirely obvious, don't worry. It'll become clear once we take a practical look at how it's done.

How to practise mindfulness

You don't have to sit still, have your eyes closed, or be in a quiet environment to practise mindfulness (although as we'll see, this can help things along). In fact, there are a variety of ways to get yourself rooted in the present – all slightly different, but achieving the same effect. Put simply, by staying focused on something that is happening *right now*, you're training yourself to spend more of your time there by default, rather than lost in thought.

In the beginning, it will be hard to clearly distinguish the difference between awareness and ordinary thought, but this is just a matter of practice. Once you've buddied up with what awareness feels like, you won't need to rely on specific portals such as the ones listed below. Awareness is like your mind operating in 'neutral', so once you're familiar with what that feels like, you'll be able to switch gears effortlessly.

For now, however, you're going to need to use one of the below methods to get yourself down the gears. The fun thing about having more than one way into the present is that you can choose your favourite! *Yeah*! Fun, right? Right? Guys?

1) Sense perceptions

By staying focused on every sensation your senses can sense, you have no choice but to stay aware of the present, since every sensation comes and goes in a matter of milliseconds.

You could have the same 'type' of sensation for an extended period – feeling cold, for example – but once you pay attention, you'll realise that the extent to which you're feeling cold is changing slightly all the time. Pay constant attention to this subtle fluctuation and you've found gateway number one into the present party.

Your breathing and heart rate are easy focal points to start with. How quickly are you breathing, and how deeply? How fast is your heart beating? Alternatively, you could try being attentive to the pressure of your slightly-too-small shoes on your toes, the clamminess of your palms, or the demands of your poor stomach to take an early lunch break. There's no need to stick to one – take your attention around the body and just notice what you notice.

Remember: don't try and work anything out or label what you feel (*'why is my heart beating so slowly/quickly, am I dying/dying?'*) or you'll lose the present. Just perceive it, that's all. Observing your sense perception, in particular the breath, is the foundation of the simple type of meditation that I'll show you later.

2) Emotions

Since they're one of the most powerful experiences us humans are subjected to, putting all of your awareness on any emotions you can feel is a great way to practise mindfulness. For example, the next time you feel anxiety or fear about something, use the emotion as a focal point, and just sit there and observe – what does being anxious *feel like*? Is it a sensation in your face, your chest, or your whole body? What can you feel that's different to when you're not anxious? The more you do this, the more you'll realise that a lot of the negativity that arises is simply a *reaction* to the sensation of anxiety, rather than to the circumstance that's making you anxious. Self-proclaimed 'spiritual entertainer' Alan Watts, who was hugely influential in introducing Eastern ideas to Western minds in the 1970's, got it spot on: *'one is a great deal less anxious if one feels perfectly free to be anxious'*.

Slowly feel the subtle presence of the anxiety, wherever and however it's manifesting, and give it permission to be there. Observe non-judgmentally long enough and you'll start to feel the gap between your awareness and the emotion it's aware of, and its grip on you will slowly diminish.

Using emotions as a way into the present moment comes with the added bonus of giving you a clearer, more balanced perspective over them, so this method comes highly recommended. By vigilantly observing your inner state you'll be denying things like anxiety, fear and anger the opportunity to overwhelm you, which is definitely one of the biggest benefits to be gained from practicing mindfulness.

3) Full acceptance of right now

A slightly different method of mindfulness practice is to sit back and let whatever happens to be happening at this point in time, happen. Consider every aspect of your experience – what sensations you can feel, where you are, who you're with, what the weather's like – and act like this is the moment your whole life has been building up to, and that you wouldn't change a thing.

Acceptance of a situation negates the constant analysis and search for improvement that is the normal state for the mind. We're wired by default to constantly pick out problems with our current situation and think about how we wish things were, even when there's nothing we can do. By wishing our surroundings were different in some way or other, we lose the present by engaging with a mental construct of some 'future' situation – one with a couple of improvements that make it superior to the present one. Full acceptance, on the other hand, logically implies that our attention is placed on what's *actually* happening in the present – and the usual mind activity that incessantly analyses, judges, categorises and resists takes a breather.

This is definitely something you've felt before, when your mind's criteria happened to have been satisfied: surrounded by your closest family and friends at your birthday dinner at Pizza Hut, you couldn't imagine any way in which the situation could be improved. Unfortunately, we usually have such strict criteria for each moment to pass that total acceptance of this type is not entirely common outside of pizza-buffet type situations.

Making a deliberate effort to give full acceptance to situations, even ones that don't satisfy our pre-existing preferences, can be a very powerful mindfulness practice. If you're stuck at an awkward ice-breaking breakfast with the awkward new interns at work, pretend that watching them awkwardly sip their coffee is the spectacle you've been waiting for all year.

The more you practise, the easier it'll become. Gradually, you'll start to get familiar with the process of letting all those judgements and labels sink into oblivion, until you're at peace with what happens, whatever it happens to be. Even if it's really, really awkward.

Good times to practise mindfulness

Let's outline a couple of typical situations where practising mindfulness is particularly convenient, just to prove that you don't have to rearrange your whole life to get started.

> *Day-to-day tasks*

Zen does not confuse spirituality with thinking about God while one is peeling potatoes. Zen spirituality is just to peel the potatoes.

Alan Watts

An easy way to schedule a bit of mindfulness into your daily routine is to give full attention to some of the things that you do anyway. By staying strictly focused on every component part of a certain action, whatever it is, you have a chance to fully root yourself in the present.

For example, a great opportunity to gently ease some mindfulness into your life is while you're eating. Instead of seeing your dinner as something to get out of the way before you can watch the kitchen TV uninhibited, really sit down and *eat that meal,* paying attention to every part and action of the process. A very useful trait for evolutionary purposes has been that we're programmed to think about the next bite of food before even finishing the current one. Try your best to resist this urge, slow down, and enjoy every bite like it's the last.

When you pick up the fork, be aware only of the feeling and weight of the fork. When you lift it to your mouth, be aware only of the arm action necessary to lift it. When you chew, be aware only of the sensation of chewing, and when you swallow... you get the idea. Not only will this multiply your appreciation of food, it's far healthier than wolfing it down, and gives you a tasty opportunity to be mindful.

A similarly great opportunity comes in those two minutes twice a day (I hope) that you're maintaining that Hollywood smile. Instead of cleaning your teeth while simultaneously having a wee, texting a friend and thinking about what you're gonna do tomorrow, just *clean your teeth*. Pick up your toothbrush like it's the first and last time you're ever going to polish those pearly whites. Concentrate while you squeeze the perfect amount of Sensodyne onto the brush (I'm assuming you're the sensitive type), notice the feeling of the brush on your teeth, and don't leave any single spot of any single tooth un-brushed.

The very least you'll come out of this experience with is a dazzlingly clean set of teeth, but if you were really trying, putting your full attention on the task will have rooted you in the present for two whole minutes. Fun fact: if you pay *really* close attention, you'll notice that the wider you open your mouth, the higher-pitched the resulting 'chuka-chuka' sound will be (although I'm as yet unsure as to whether mouthing the tune to Match of the Day to yourself in the mirror constitutes genuine mindfulness practice).

> *When drifting into the abyss*

One of the most beneficial ways to use mindfulness is as a natural sleep aid. You may have previously been advised to slowly take your attention around the body if you're struggling to get some shut-eye, and this technique is mindfulness through and through.

Next time you're lying frustrated in bed, instead of counting sheep for an hour, get some mindfulness practice in. Lie as comfortably as you can, and then start to try and 'feel' your left foot. It may seem difficult to begin with, but give it a minute of pure focus and you'll become acutely aware of your foot in much the same way that a recipient of local anaesthetic is acutely unaware of theirs.

Once you've 'ticked it off', move onto the next foot, then gradually move your attention around each part of the body until you can *feel* it. You'll notice that once you gain awareness of a couple of body parts in a row, you can 'flow' your attention between them, which is just about one of the most pleasant sensations that you can experience with your clothes on. This is a form of meditation in itself and will work wonders in calming your mind and rooting you in the present, while simultaneously helping you to drop off.

> *Waiting for stuff*

Our natural response to being made to wait for something – stuck in traffic, waiting for our computer to boot up, in line at the post office – is to feel agitated, check our watches, and curse the woman at the counter for taking over five minutes to stamp one bit of paper. This causes a heap of unnecessary suffering, since after all, waiting for stuff is an inevitable and inescapable part of day-to-day life. One of the easiest ways to fit in some mindfulness practice is through these gaps – you're stuck in the present anyway, so you may as well keep your attention there.

If your friend has texted to say that they're going to be late for the sixth consecutive week to your Friday night bingo session, instead of waiting impatiently and giving them the evil eye when they finally arrive, be grateful that you've had a chance to practise mindfulness. Just stand or sit there, not 'waiting' for anything, but instead just being aware – of your inner state, of the passing cars, of the muffled ball announcements coming from within the hall.

Start to notice the unique, fluctuating characteristics of each individual passing moment, and you'll see your mindset shift from 'hurry up for god's sake, we're missing numbers!' towards 'don't worry babe, take your time'. Start to appreciate life's pauses as a chance to get into the present, and you'll wonder why you ever made 'being made to wait' into a negative.

> *Sitting on public transport*

Since it's something that most of us have to 'get through' daily to arrive at or return from various destinations, sitting on the bus/train/tram is a perfect time to just sit there and be mindful until you reach your stop. Notice the hum of the engine, the non-existent hum of conversation between your fellow train passengers, and the hum of the slightly odd man on your left who you suspect has just been sat humming on the train for the last 6 days.

On the way into work, you'll find that you're putting yourself in a great state of mind for a productive day, and on the way back, you'll find that you walk through your front door already half-unwound, ready to make the most of the remaining half-hour of your evening.

> *Learning how to do things*

Finally, if you happen to be learning a new skill, you can kill two birds with one stone by turning mind-numbing repetition into mindfulness practice. For example, if you were practicing scales on your beloved trumpet: instead of blasting through it wishing that the 30 minutes you promised yourself per day was already over, focus completely on every slight movement and sensation of your fingers, mouth and lungs, nailing every note as perfectly and accurately as you can. You'll achieve a still mind, and what's more, you'll be conditioning yourself to play with utmost accuracy. With a focused, mindful attitude towards practice, the path towards musical mastery (or anything mastery) will cease to be a chore.

What's the best way to practise?

The above methods are just childsplay when compared to the undisputed king of present-practice. Before we go ahead and get stuck into solving some of life's problems with the helping hand of mindfulness, you're going to need to know how its golden goose gets the job done. Get excited – I'm about to arm you with the most powerful and effective technique you'll ever find for taming your mind.

Meditation – A Practical Guide

"It feels just like it should"

Jamiroquai

"Meditation is not about feeling a certain way. It's about feeling the way you feel."

Jon Kabat-Zinn, Mindfulness scientist (in response, maybe)

As we've just seen, mindfulness can be practised pretty much anywhere, at any time, whatever you're doing. While all of the benefits can slowly come to you with day-to-day practice, if you're really serious about taming your mind, it's best to get some *meditation* hours under your belt. Meditation can be described as a slightly more formal and methodical practice of mindfulness –by putting yourself in the environment most conducive to maintaining a mindful state, you're putting yourself in the best position to fast-track your progress.

The images your mind might have conjured about meditation may have included, but not been limited to, being *'seated in an unbearable cross-legged position in a room that smelled like feet, with a group of smug 'practitioners' ringing bells, ogling crystals, intoning om, and attempting to float off into some sort of cosmic goo'*, a pretty accurate account of the average set of preconceptions by ABC news anchor Dan

Harris. In fact, it's an incredibly simple practice – if anything, too simple, which is why it's accumulated so much useless baggage over the years (which we're going to ignore completely).

Mindfulness meditation, if practised correctly, simply involves sitting down, trying to stay in the present by focusing on something that's happening right now, and taking your attention back to that thing whenever your mind starts to wander. After you notice a thought has grabbed your attention away from its intended target, you don't kick up a fuss, but politely and gently take your attention back. All concepts of good, bad, happy, and sad are put to one side for a period of time, allowing the truth – by which I mean the *raw data* of experience, that which is *undeniably* occurring – to arise without being muddied by concepts and value judgements like it usually is.

It's sort of like shutting down your mind-PC (*yes, it's back*). Slowly, you'll become aware of each of your thoughts (running programs), and as soon as you notice them, let them go on their merry way (slowly closing them down) and return your attention to the breath. With practice, it'll be quicker and quicker to end every process until they only appear very occasionally – and in the gaps that appear, all that remains is awareness.

Of course, when you finish your meditation, your computer will start up again, and so will the programs. However, if you continue to cultivate mindfulness, you'll start to habitually spend more of your time with Task Manager open. This doesn't mean that it's *bad* to have thoughts, and that we're trying to eradicate them all together – but just like running programs, it's nice to keep tabs on them from a distance rather than letting them dominate completely[1].

Although meditation is one of the simplest hobbies around, you're not going to have much luck trying to wing it without reading the instructions. The best choice for beginners is to have a go at what is arguably the most common type of meditation – focusing on the breath.

Quick-start guide

1) Find a quiet (ish) room.

You're going to be practicing not getting distracted by your thoughts, so the addition of your housemate playing acid-house-techno-gypsy-electro-swing at full volume in the room next door is probably going to be a bit too much to handle. However, don't get caught putting off a session just because there's a little bit of traffic noise, or someone's watching TV three houses down – silence is not a necessity.

2) Sit down.

---

[1] Admittedly, I prepared an extension of this analogy regarding *Defragmenting Your Mind,* but I think I'd run the risk of losing those of you who stuck with me through *Task Manage*r..

You may have thought that meditation necessarily involves getting on the floor and tangling up your legs as though they were made of spaghetti. Not true – whatever position is the most comfortable for you is the best way. Cross legged on a sturdy cushion on the floor is ideal, but on a chair is completely fine too. Give it a bit of trial and error and see what works for you.

Keep your back straight in the same way you would when standing in correct posture – as though a taut string is glued to the top-middle of your head, pulling you up just enough to keep you straight and balanced, but no tighter. With your hands, do whatever feels comfortable.

These guidelines are to encourage a position that'll be stable and safe during longer sessions, but feel free to be creative, since it's what's going on in your head that counts. You could even lie down if you really fancy it, but there's a very good chance your twenty minute sit will turn into a hundred minute nap.

3) Set a timer.

At the very beginning, you can start with 5 minutes, but you'll get more benefit by gradually increasing this as you go along. 20 minutes a day is plenty, and is a routine that should fit well into any lifestyle (however, as a general rule, the more you sit the better). Don't peek at the timer before it goes off, and if you find yourself begging to be saved by the bell, try to practise being *aware* of that desire rather than getting carried away by it.

4) Close your eyes.

It's best to shut your eyes, since the mind has a tendency to go in all sorts of crazy directions from even the slightest bit of sensory input. For me, looking at the peeling skirting board and the holes in the walls of my bedroom tends to make me wonder why I have not yet moved into a nicer house, which can be a big distraction[1].

5) Put all of your attention on your breathing

Breathing through your nose, notice the sensations of the breathing process wherever you can feel them most distinctly – it will likely be the gentle feeling of the air passing in and out of your nostrils. At first, your awareness of this area will be vague and hazy, but the longer you keep your attention there, the more distinct the sensations will be.

Try and notice each inhalation and exhalation as soon as it starts, following it all the way through until the last vibrations and sensations of each breath have finished. Don't try and control the breath, instead, just try to go along with whatever it was going to do anyway. This can be tricky at first, but try

[1] If you're feeling particularly compassionate after your session, I am not too proud to accept donations above and beyond the price of this book.

your best to relinquish control, letting your body breathe how it wants, as though you were asleep.

Keeping your attention on an anchor like this is like putting stabilisers on your bike (except it doesn't make you less cool). There's nothing particularly special about the breath – if you wanted to, you could ride around in awareness freestyle for a little while, paying attention to each and every sensation as it arose. However, it's much easier to fall off the bike and get lost in thought that way, so we pick something convenient that's happening *now* to give us a bit of balance.

6) Bring your attention back whenever you get distracted

Pretty much anything can distract you from your focus of the breath – a thought, a sensation, an emotion, a thought about a sensation, an emotion about a thought. Brace yourself for the fact that it's going to happen, a *lot*. You'll more than likely stay focused on the breath for two seconds, think 'this is easy!', then before you know it realise you've just spent five minutes mentally planning out the contents of the sandwich you're having for lunch. Make sure not to get down about it – getting distracted and starting again is where you're doing the 'rep' and building your mindfulness muscle. It figures that in the beginning the muscle will be relatively weak, so don't worry if you find yourself doing regular reps.

This is where the actual work is done, so don't see frequent distractions as some kind of obstacle to be surmounted before you can meditate properly. Don't worry about getting distracted, and don't judge yourself when you are. Just gently take your attention back to your breath. *Rinse and repeat until enlightened.*

This is the essence of meditation, and it is not easy. When asking your thinking mind whether it would like to be escorted out the easy way, or by kicking and screaming, it always chooses the latter. However, the difficulty of meditation is not an inherent feature of the practice – it's a feature of the mind you're trying to tame, and only when you attempt to meditate for the first time will you realise how hyperactive your mind really is. Take heart in the knowledge that before you started meditating, your mind was just as crazy as it is now – at least now you're looking that insanity square in the eye. The mind is a worthy opponent, and there will be a fight, but it's one you will win if you persevere.

Before moving on, I advise having a go at following the instructions, even if only for 2 minutes – the rest of the chapter will make a lot more sense to you if you do. Put down this book, sit comfortably in your chair, and put all your attention on your breathing. When you noticed a thought has taken your attention away, observe the arising of the thought, then return your attention to the breath. Go do it for a few minutes.

If you're reading *this* sentence, and you *still* haven't had a little try at meditation as instructed above, *please* go back and do so (three lots of italics in one sentence, so you know I'm serious). You'll get a lot more out of the rest of the chapter if you have even just a little bit of personal experience to relate it to.

How often, and how long?

Progress in meditation is simply measured by the hours you've racked up with bum-on-cushion, so the answer is, 'as often and as long as possible'. However, it's far better to create a reasonable routine that you'll actually stick to than an overly ambitious one that you won't.

Just like most things in life, the secret of success is consistent practice, and just like learning the Jazz flute, 10 minutes of meditation once a day is far more effective than 3 hours every Sunday. For the first week, just sit for 5 minutes as soon as you wake up every day. For the second week, go for 10 minutes. The third week, 15 minutes, fourth, 20 minutes. This should ease you into a good routine. Yeah, so you may have to only hit snooze twice instead of three times to make some time, but keep it up and you'll see that it's more than worth the sacrifice.

It can be helpful to lead up to your session with a few things that calm you down. If your head's all over the place and you can tell that meditation is going to be very difficult, just relax, pour yourself a cuppa, and listen to your *'well chilled'* playlist for a while before starting. Having said that, don't catch yourself endlessly putting off sessions because you're a little stressed – meditation is your best bet for reaching a better state of mind anyway, so get your bum on that cushion, and you'll feel a lot better for it.

What's the best time to meditate?

There is arguably no bad time to meditate, as long as you have a suitable environment to do it in. However, most sources (including this one) will tell you that the best time is first thing in the morning. This is because your mind will be fresh from rest and won't have had too much input to process for a while – this way, you can get to a level of calm in 10 minutes that could take you an hour during the day. A morning session also gives you a great opportunity to become aware of everything that's floating around in your mind before you head out into the world – anything that is important for the day ahead will be sure to make an appearance during that early twenty-minute sit, so you can get up off the cushion feeling calm, relaxed, and ready for the day.

Likewise, a quick burst of meditation during your lunch break at work is a great way to centre yourself after a stressful morning and set yourself up for a productive afternoon. In fact, shortly *after* your main activity of the day (work, study, fishing) is also a great time to meditate, as it'll encourage the processing of the day's events and enable you to have a nice relaxing night in without your work/coursework/fish problems barging their way into your attention.

I think you get the idea – the best time to meditate is the time you can find.

What to expect

The instinctive reaction to unexpected happenings while meditating is usually *'I bet this happens to nobody else, so I guess this business just isn't for me'* . Hopefully by pre-warning you, you'll be prepared for when these happenings happen to happen.

1) Being lost in thought for the whole session

The number one thing to remember is that meditation is *not* an overnight success kind of deal. In the beginning, don't expect your sessions to be fun in any way, shape, or form. In fact, they will probably be absolutely *not fun*.

In total contrast to what you may imagine as a walk in the park, meditation is more like attempting to climb up a telegraph pole smothered in Vaseline (I'll let your imagination decide whether it's you or the pole that's smothered). Anyone who tells you otherwise is either not doing it properly or lying to you. Don't worry if your first several (or dozen) (or several dozen) attempts end up with you sat there lost in thought for 20 minutes. It happens to everyone, and is a phase that every Zen master has been through too.

With time, however, you'll notice that instead of an endless stream of thoughts, small gaps of pure awareness (where you remain focused on the contents of the present) begin to become a feature of your practice. Thoughts will still arise, but they will seem quieter, 'wispier', and you'll be able to watch them rise and fall without getting caught up in them.

The best advice I can give you is to take it one breath at a time. Always resolve that you will stay aware for this, singular, current breath: forget about trying to stay focused for the whole session, instead just keeping your awareness on the inhalation or exhalation that's happening *right now*. You will still get distracted on a regular basis, but if you persevere with the resolve to focus on the current breath, this will eventually add up into longer periods of awareness.

2) Boredom, frustration, wishing it was over

You'll find that the most common experiences at the beginning are boredom and frustration, which often combine into a sort of 'this is bullshit' resistance that implores you to get up off the cushion. Also common is 'how on earth has it not been 10 minutes already?', in which case your disbelief may lead you to peek at your timer, at which point it will inform you that it has, indeed, not been 10 minutes already.

Wishing your time away during meditation, just like you might do during a slow Tuesday at work, is the opposite of what we're trying to practise – so make sure to catch yourself whenever it's happening. We're so often in the habit of wishing the present moment would just go away (so that a superior future one would come around) that we can spend our whole lives *waiting* to be content. Use meditation to work on just trying to accept, or even *enjoy*, the moment you're in, even if you're bored as hell, and you'll find the effect leaks rather effectively into those slow Tuesdays.

It's worth noting here that it's far easier to be motivated to practise meditation when things are going *well* than when they aren't. When your mind is good mates with the current circumstances of your life, meditation is a lot more pleasant, and you're a lot more likely to keep up the practice. Conversely, when the shit is hitting the fan, the mind starts throwing a tantrum, and it can be hard to take a step back.

However, keeping up your practice when you're in a bit of a trough is arguably far more beneficial than just meditating throughout the good times. The more you practise acceptance of your shit-covered fan before the tides of time wash it clean, the more you'll find that peace of mind takes less of a hit the next time things take a downward turn.

3) Physical pain and discomfort

Sitting in a position you haven't really sat in before for 20 minutes in a row without moving is probably going to hurt something, eventually. Ideally, stay objective with any sensation whatsoever, however unpleasant, and use it as a subject of your awareness. Eventually you'll recognise that a not-insignificant portion of the pain we experience in general is mind-made, and stems from our mind instinctively going 'err.. NOPE' to any slight discomfort and making a big fuss of it. By keeping your focus on the *raw data* of the pain and staying objective, a gap will grow between you and your negative reaction to it, and you'll start to experience it as just another sensation, neither good nor bad.

Don't worry – as long as you're sitting with good posture, you're not doing any long term damage, your body is just getting used to a new position[1].

4) Insights and realisations

It's helpful to picture meditation as a spring cleaning for the mind – by clearing out the cobwebs we can end up finding some goodies down there. When we reduce the extent to which our old stock of thoughts are dominating our consciousness, we're freeing up room for all sorts of new and unique stuff to arise from deeper down. I can only speak

----

[1] Unless of course you have pre-existing problems with your knees or back, in which case you should probably check with the doc before going full-lotus for three hours.

from personal experience, but for me it's been conclusive that the longer the gap I manage between thoughts, the higher *quality* of the thoughts that pop up.

It's pretty interesting to start to become familiar with what's buried underneath the flurry of day-to-day concerns that usually occupy all of our attention. By creating a little space in our conscious attention, new insights will have an easier time floating up from below instead of being refused an entry point by the non-stop whizzing of normal thought. For example, the problems that your subconscious was working on may start to float to the surface – and it's not uncommon to stumble upon an insight about, or solution to, something you'd been vaguely curious or concerned about for a while.

I regularly finish a session with a cool new idea about something that I can't wait to act on. This can be pretty distracting if it comes to you towards the beginning of the session, because your mind will be begging you to stand up and go write it down, but don't worry – it will be waiting patiently for you once you finish up and get to a notepad.

5) Stillness, peace of mind, and all that jazz

With meditation you give yourself a better chance than day-to-day mindfulness of staying in the present for longer, and the bigger proportion of your sit that you manage to stay there, the more you could be in store for a big helping of stillness and peace. The state is difficult to describe, but it's generally accepted that there is some sort of pleasurable 'tone' to the experience of pure awareness without thought. This feeling isn't generated by anything, it's one that's uncovered.

Getting into a mental state where we can simply be attentive to our experience without constantly judging and categorising it is the equivalent of treating the mind, which spends most of its time on the treadmill at the highest speed, to a soak in a bubble bath. When we're rooted in right now, the usual relentless stream of thought becomes slightly more relenting – and having the noisy processes of the mind switched off, even for a brief moment, is really, really, really nice.

You won't always encounter tangible feelings of peace, but I can honestly say that on my end, I genuinely feel 'better' after every single sit, even if very slightly. If you ever get that 'lost' feeling, where you're not sure what to do with yourself in the next hour, week or even year, a good meditation sit will always lend a hand in steering you in the right direction and easing your mind. Having spent half an hour in the present (or at least trying to be), the incessant and largely ineffective worries about the past or the future will have lost some of their dominance, with the peace of the present sneaking in as a replacement.

The most important thing to remember

It was a bit irresponsible of me to go on about feeling 'peaceful' in the previous paragraph – getting caught seeking to achieve pleasant sensations and avoid unpleasant ones is one of the biggest potential pitfalls for a fledgling meditator. Instinctively, you're going to sit there and mentally label everything that happens, especially how 'well' the session is going, and it can be tempting to start labelling your meditation sessions as good or bad, productive or unproductive. Experience a big helping of stillness or peace and you could get caught trying to replicate that sensation from then on – and if future sessions don't live up to what you experienced, you won't be satisfied.

Remember: as an objective observer, there *is* no good or bad, and stillness should get no more approval than frustration. The benefits of meditation come through looking at the reality of the mind, not from achieving any particular state or other, so an agitated session is just as good as a pleasant one.

Funnily enough, due to the hyperactivity of 'seeking' something, the more you crave specific sensations in this way, the more they will elude you. Wishing that your mind would calm down is only going to result in the opposite, so try to make friends with literally anything that's happening during the session, remembering that you're just there to observe it non-judgmentally.

You're sitting to observe the reality of your mind as it is, rather than how you wish it would be – so if the reality is that your mind is all over the place, that's totally fine. Let what wants to come up come up, then let it float on as you return attention to the breath. That's all you need to do. Stop looking for peace of mind, and that's when you'll stumble upon it.

Hit me with your best shot

Meditation is your best hope of making some headway in your fight to take some control back from the mind. Although day-to-day mindfulness can bring the same benefits, it'll take a lot longer if you don't also set aside the time to sit down and really start to observe the mind, free of other distractions.

By giving you a small-scale battle ground for undoing the deep rooted mechanisms of good-craving and bad-resisting, meditation provides a perfect practise opportunity for staying objective with the ups and downs of daily life. Use meditation to draw some of the judgmental, emotional charge out of what you experience, and the effect will leak into your everyday existence. Start off with accepting the subtle pain in your arse, and it'll spread to acceptance of that pain in the arse at work, and it'll keep scaling upward.

Think of it like the homework you had at school. Meditation gives you some exercises to complete at home, which will prepare you for when it really matters – in the *examination of life*. Just like any homework, don't expect it to be easy, and don't expect it to be fun – but give it a month and you won't know how you managed to stay sane without it.

——

This brings the practical section to a close, but don't worry about memorising what we've covered here – you can find a concise summary of the practical instructions in the Appendix in the back.

For now, let's take a deeper dive into the functioning of the mind, using what we've learnt in the last few chapters to make a couple of tune-ups.

Part 2: Mechanisms Of The Mind

The mind, we sometimes forget, is just another functional body part. Just like our heads, our shoulders, our knees and our toes, it provides a service for us (thinking). Just like the others, it's prone to malfunctioning – the key difference being that while we're perfectly aware when our head is bleeding, our shoulder has dislocated, our knees are creaking or our toe is broken, we're largely oblivious to the extent to which our mind systematically negates all of our hard efforts for happiness.

This is because on first impressions, it seems as though we have control over the mind: it seems like we deliberately think our thoughts, and decide our reactions to things. This simply isn't true – we have no control over what thoughts come up, and which emotions get generated. They just happen.

If we really had control, why would we choose to think negative thoughts, or let negative emotions arise? The mind just receives its input, interprets it, and produces its output. This all happens without our consent, with thoughts and emotions rising and falling constantly. If we can't control it, but it can control us, then it looks like we're actually the slave, and it's our master. Either way, we shouldn't think that ourselves and our mind activity are one and the same.

This case of mistaken identity is considered completely normal, due to the fact that it's an affliction many of us suffer from and are oblivious to. It arises because the mind produces thoughts pretty relentlessly throughout our waking lives, and our attention is placed on these thoughts for the majority of the time. This doesn't happen out of choice, but simply because thoughts are very loud and obtrusive, and grab our attention as soon as they appear. As a result, we feel like those thoughts are the only obvious choice to derive our sense of identity from, when in fact, they're just random spazzes of the brain.

We don't have to stand for it. The mind should be ours to boss about. Luckily, given the right tools, we can start to organise a heroic coup d'état.

In this section, we're going to be learning to:

> Reveal the biggest trick played on us by our minds

> Take a look at the irrational and hapless ways we look for fulfilment

> Uproot the foundations of our self-esteem from the sand on which they're built, drive inland a little, and build them on stone instead

Make sure to keep your thinking caps *off* for this one.

Joe, meet Joe's ego

Spending most of our time engaged with our thoughts fools us into feeling like there's a little person who lives behind our eyes, drives our body, thinks our thoughts, and experiences our experiences. This little person is that narrating voice in our heads, commenting on everything that happens, and as it happens, we're convinced that we *are* that little person.

Think right now about your favourite flavour of ice-cream, and notice who it is that seems to tell you the answer – that's who we're getting at. That wispy inner monologue is the *ego*, also referred to as the *self*, as in, it ends up being what we see as our-*selves*.

We end up thinking that this inner monologue is us for a couple of reasons. Firstly, it can be so dominant in our mental space that it becomes impossible not to follow it, with our thoughts screaming for attention like a hungry toddler craving a sundae. Being carried away by our mental activity all day makes it seem like we're in some way controlling its direction, but this simply isn't true. The fact that we can get 'lost in thought', then 'wake up' two minutes later, is enough to show that we're not pulling the strings here – the monologue isn't us.

Secondly, it even *sounds* like us – the voice of that internal narrator is generally identical to the one that comes out of our mouths when we speak. This fools us into identifying with it, but really, this inner monologue is just as 'us' as anything else we experience, like when we've got a song stuck playing in our head. In fact, a noise playing in our heads without our consent is all that the inner monologue really is – it arises of its own accord, plays its tune for a little while, then goes away again.

However, once it goes away, it's not long before it seems to pop up again – and this is the biggest reason for our identification with it. Once our internal monologue dies down for a few seconds, a highly similar (but slightly different) one comes back just moments later to replace it – so it seems like there's a consistent 'person' that's along for the ride, when in fact the monologue is freshly generated each time.

To illustrate, consider one of those cartoon flip books. Every page displays only a slight change from the last one, so when you flip between them rapidly it gives the illusion of there being a singular, consistent man dancing around, jumping through hoops and getting up to all sorts of crazy adventures. In fact, we all know that every flip of the page involves the absolute annihilation of the previous man, and a rebirth of an entirely new one, but because it's flipping quickly, the illusion is upheld.

And so it is with the little person in our heads, the one that seems to be thinking our thoughts. We feel like we're the same person when we go to sleep at night as when we wake up in the morning, but when you think about it, what is it exactly that *survived* the night's sleep? When we wake up, the narrator that makes sense of it all has changed. The new *self* is just a random spaz of the brain to start off the day. A new one is born every morning, every hour, in fact, every moment.

There *is* no consistent thinker. Thoughts just rise and fall in consciousness without our consent, and so does the feeling of the thinker itself. This feeling of a *self* is just another transitory thought, another fleeting experience. This impression given to us by this apparent continuity, that there is a stable *self* that remains constant from day to day, is the biggest trick played on us by our minds.

Noticing this game at play requires a bit of practice: the answer eludes us because it's right under our nose. We are often so identified with the inner monologue that it can be hard to take a step back from it.

Not to worry. It'll take a bit of practice, but conveniently, mindfulness gives us all of the introspective tools we'll need to up our game.

Give it some of the 'm' word

"Start by being fully aware of what you think you are. It'll help you to become aware of what you are in fact."

Aldous Huxley

The fact that the feeling of the *self* is just another experience means that it's something that we can step back from by moving our attention resolutely back to the present – onto the ledge behind the waterfall.

By using mindfulness to create a gap between our awareness and what it's aware of, the impression of a *thinker* of the thoughts, and *experiencer* of the sensations, is revealed to be just as transient and flimsy as the thoughts and sensations themselves. With practice, the idea that we could possibly *be* one of these thoughts, or a stream of them, is shown to be unjustifiable.

Undoing our identification from the *self* happens naturally when we practise any type of mindfulness – that is, as long as we spend time keeping our awareness on something that's actually happening in the present, rather than being carried away by our mind activity. However, it's also possible to go about it a little more deliberately.

For example, next time you're practicing meditation, put your attention on the experience of the internal monologue whenever it arises, trying your best to stay separate from it without letting it carry you away. Notice how the feeling of *being* that thinker is just another feeling, another sensation, that rises in consciousness then falls away. Keep up your practice and it will slowly become apparent that there is no concrete, lasting *self* to be found anywhere.

What remains when that feeling of *self* is diminished is awareness itself: that which is still there *in-between* thoughts, emotions and experiences. It's the ledge behind the waterfall, the only thing that's ever-present. It's that which is *aware* of the thoughts we have, but knows that it isn't them, in the same way that we're aware that we have an itch on our arm or leg, but don't go through life feeling like we *are* those itches.

By using mindfulness techniques to spend more time on this ledge, it becomes clear that the extent to which our sense of *self* dominates our attention can be reduced. With practice, the monologue will still pop up regularly, but it will seem a little quieter, and be less likely to carry us away on a magic carpet ride of compulsive thought.

The fact that the domination of the inner monologue can be lessened is proof in itself that it isn't us – if the feeling of a *self* was who we were, could we really 'erase ourselves' by practicing mindfulness? No chance – by practicing mindfulness we're uncovering our true identity, not doing away with it. The ledge behind the waterfall of our experience is the only thing that we're always going to have – so it's a far better HQ to base our identity in than the comings and goings of the mind.

This is not to say that the sense of *self* should be entirely demolished and that we should reside in pure awareness. If we can instead manage to accept the sense of *self* while not letting it dominant proceedings, this results in a far better arrangement, and one that's conducive to a happier state.

To find out why, let's first have a look at a couple features of the ego, of the *self*, and see how they conspire to prevent us from reaching peace of mind.

You're insecure, I know what for

It seems obvious that the stimulus that enters the brain will largely determine what we end up thinking about – spend 12 hours playing Solitaire on your phone, and you'll probably find that you can't help but move playing cards about in your mind's eye for the rest of the day.

Taking it one step further, the bundle of information that we've been given to interpret since birth is undoubtedly going to influence the ego that's formed as a result. Taking it one more step further, it figures that the society we get this information from, and live our lives surrounded by, will have a huge impact on the characteristics of the ego. In fact, the ego ends up pretty much soaking up all of its motives, values and desires from its surroundings in this way.

When we take a look at what kind of things the Western culture places a high value on, it's not difficult to see why identifying too much with the ego only serves to make us suffer. For example, our society places quite a lot of emphasis on 'doing well' in the eyes of everybody else, and largely equates self-worth to how much we've achieved, and how much we have. It's no mystery that this kind of information only serves to instil in us an underlying feeling of discontent, and the nagging feeling that we should always be improving ourselves, getting more, and achieving more. The inevitable result is an insecure ego obsessed with having lots of stuff, comparing itself to others, and crafting a life that looks good from the outside.

If our identification with the ego is left unchecked, we risk gearing almost of our actions towards making sure this little 'me' in our heads feels as good about itself as possible. When our biggest motivator is making sure everything looks good from the outside, we end up spending half of our time frantically keeping up a hundred spinning plates of self-image. When most of our actions have the aim of keeping up appearances, we end up living by values that aren't even our own, and it's no wonder that this only brings suffering.

Some of the most common results of spending our lives driven by upholding this self-image are:

> toning down any 'out-there' behaviours, actions or ambitions in order to escape possible judgement
> striving to make sure everyone is aware of our achievements, while ignorant to our failures
> maintaining the appearance of having everything under control at all times, for example by keeping up a 'brave face'

around our family and friends, instead of asking for help when we need it

This is a life lived through ego, and it's a total drag. Needing to constantly win the million little battles of self-image is a blatant sign that we're losing the war, with our self-esteem about as secure as a sailing knot tied with silly string.

They call me the seeker

This insecurity also has a number of consequences – most notably that we always feel 'incomplete', constantly looking for this or that to improve our situation, yet never satisfied for long when we find it.

An inevitable result of growing up in a society where tangible, external success is prioritised is that when we're feeling discontent, it seems like that some kind of external improvement must hold the solution – a more rewarding job, a better looking spouse, a cooler hairdo. We're always working to try and find whatever it is that we think is missing, hoping that it'll fill the void and remove our discontent – and as a result we're constantly in 'seeking' mode.

Unfortunately, if our drive to make, get or achieve stems from trying to solve a nagging internal insecurity or discontent, we may well make, get or achieve what we were looking for, but it'll never solve the inner feeling of unfulfilment. This is because it's not the absolute characteristics of our wants and desires that make us want them – it's because it's in the wiring of an eternally insecure ego to *want to want* more than we actually *want to have*. Unless we change our ways, the cycle will never stop.

Each time there's a belief that just 'one more win' is all we'd need to be rid of our discontent – *if only I found a partner/had a better work-life balance/won the lottery, I'd be happy*. When we get that thing and reach that higher level of satisfaction, we may experience the 'yes, I made it!' sensation for a little while, but it always fades eventually. It's a temporary high based on a superficial gain. We adjust to our new situation until it becomes standard, and the feeling of incompleteness starts to creep back in. At this point our mind slowly moves up the gears again to figure out what it needs next.

The result of this cycle of endless seeking and temporary satisfaction is that even though everything may end up looking great on paper, there's always something more to be gained. There's no arbitrary level of success that we can reach that magically undoes the 'seeking' mode of the ego, so without breaking out of the same old patterns, our dream circumstances will never be satisfactory even if we manage to achieve them. The ego doesn't realise that this nasty seeking habit *is* the problem, and that unless it changes its ways, the feeling of incompleteness will never kindly gather its things and go away.

The implication is as follows: blindly making, getting, and achieving *more* with the vague assumption that one day we'll have made, gotten, or achieved enough to be happy is not going to work. The ego's satisfaction bucket is leaky, so we'll never be able to fill it by just pouring in a load of water.

The psychology world refers to this as the *hedonic treadmill*. There's a temporary increase in satisfaction when we reach what we perceive as a 'higher level', but we always return to our baseline happiness eventually – a result found in countless empirical studies on those who received big external 'wins', like lottery winners[viii]. As we'll see, mindfulness does not imply that we shouldn't have a go at reaching peak experiences occasionally, but instead teaches us that increasing the baseline should definitely be the priority.

It's clear that the quality of our experience is almost entirely determined by what's going on inside, not by what we have on the outside. It therefore makes sense that our *response* to the circumstances of our lives is where we should be focusing our attention, rather than just blindly striving to improve those circumstances.

Before we find out how we go about doing this, there's one last mechanism of the mind for us to take a look at.

I just wanna be yours

As we've just seen, the ego is endlessly looking for the hidden piece of the puzzle, the elusive external condition that will end our insecurity and make us feel content. When we find something and that hit of satisfaction comes, boy, what a lovely feeling that is. The kind of feeling you never want to leave you. And what do you do when you don't want something to leave you? You hold on, *tight*.

Attachment occurs when the insecure little 'me' inside our heads becomes reliant on the existence of one or more external conditions in order to maintain this feeling of security. As we'll see, this turns out to be a pretty silly game plan in a world where both the internals and externals are hell-bent on changing all the time.

One of the deepest foundations of Buddhism is that all suffering is caused by attaching to things in this way. Our problems are caused by being attached to having certain things around, or having certain things go a certain way, and the more we're attached to, the more we're increasing our reliance on externals to feel content.

Once attachment happens, the existence of the condition, whatever it is, starts to play a part in how secure the ego feels – and this works both ways. If it stays around, we feel good, but if it goes, we mourn the loss. Buddhist teacher

Kelsang Gyatso raises the example of having an attachment to your car:

When our car, for example, has a problem we usually say 'I have a problem', but in reality it is the car's problem and not our problem. The car's problem is an outer problem, and our problem, which is our unpleasant feeling, is an inner problem. These two problems are completely different. We need to solve the car's problem by repairing it, and we need to solve our own problem by controlling our attachment to the car.

Most of the time, we're so identified with the insecure ego that the majority of our actions are geared towards forming and maintaining these attachments, and it never ends. We go through life granting a thousand things the ability to make us feel miserable – yet we continue to form attachments regardless, because that feeling of 'not enough' *still* hasn't gone away. Unfortunately for the ego, no number of attachments is going to satiate its insecurity (for long), and unfortunately for us, the ego doesn't realise this. So it goes on attaching like it's goin' outta fashion.

One of the most common types of attachments is to the characteristics of our ego, of our self-image: the things that make us feel like 'us'. We build up a mental image of ourselves, and although such an image is never going to get close to the totality of who we are, we go through life incredibly attached to it. Just like all the other attachments we make, this isn't a great idea, and only serves to make us miserable.

For example, our attachment to our appearance is a really common one – think back to a time in your life where after some kind of miscommunication you ended up with a really, really awful haircut. You couldn't bear to look at yourself in the mirror, and even when riding the bus home, you felt incredibly self-conscious, as though everybody looking at you *knew* you'd just had an awful haircut. This suffering occurs because our current appearance is such a big part of what we think of as *us* that when it's bad, we feel bad, as though we're one and the same.

In reality, the precise arrangement of the hairs on our heads hardly captures much of who we are as a whole – yet because of attachment to our appearance, we feel diminished when they don't happen to fall into a nice formation. The fact that we actually feel *worse* when we're having a bad hair day is proof enough that such an attachment is doomed to cause us misery.

To further illustrate how clinging to characteristics in this way make us suffer, let's introduce a friendly hypothetical character, Attachment Andy. Here are some of the ways in which Andy sees himself:

> Always well-dressed and looking sharp
> Gets a pretty decent pay packet
> Knows more about Star Wars than pretty much everyone

Andy's attached to the above conditions in order to build up his self-image, and make himself feel more secure. This isn't to say that Andy isn't well paid, doesn't dress fairly well, and hasn't seen the entire Star Wars saga back to back sixteen times. The problem is that by attaching to an idea of himself that only exists in his head, Andy's building the foundations of his identity on a load of sand, which could just blow away any minute now. Although the reason behind making attachments is to reduce feelings of insecurity, all they end up doing is building a big sense of self on a flimsy foundation. To show why, have a think about what would happen if all of this happened in one day:

> Someone asked Andy if he was 'really going out in that awful shirt', before he was headed to the pub
> After a few drinks, all of his friends revealed that they actually earn twice his salary
> He failed to win the knockout round of the pub quiz, when the topic was *"Late 20th century science-fiction films by big hairy directors"*

How would you feel if you were Attachment Andy right now? Not great – in fact, he probably feels shaken to the core. Since he was attached to those three conditions and using them to form his self-image, part of what he thinks of as 'himself' has now been diminished, and you wouldn't blame him for having a little cry in the toilets after such a big blow.

When we derive our identity by attaching to external conditions, which have the common feature of invariably coming and going, suffering is the inevitable consequence. It's like trying to anchor a boat to a lump of seaweed that's at any moment just going to up and float away. When the basis for our identity is constantly fluctuating, we never get the security from our attachments that we were looking for, but we grant them free reign on causing us suffering anyway.

Funnily enough, being a 'cynic' is an identity people *love* to take on, and is probably part of the reason that you picked up this book (thanks *Marketing 101*!). You'd probably hate it if one of your friends mentioned in passing that you're one of the least cynical people he knows, because being a cynic is pretty cool, as characteristics go. You see yourself as a cynic, which makes you feel good, but when that attachment is challenged, you feel the burn.

It's important to clarify that not being attached to the things in our lives doesn't reduce our appreciation for them – we just enjoy them while they're around and accept them for what they are, without needing to rely on them to feel secure. It's common sense that it's far healthier to enjoy our ever-changing relationship with these conditions while they last, without trying to gain from them something that they cannot offer. In an attachment-free life, when the time has come for some condition to float on out of our lives, we're able to let it go gracefully, with gratitude for the time it was there.

As we'll find out, if we get in touch with the part of us that doesn't come and go, we lose the need to attach to the things that do.

Let it go, let it go..

In this chapter we've looked at three classic characteristics of the egoic mind: insecurity, seeking, and attachment. By identifying with the ego, we're tricked into believing that our feelings of discontent must be caused by a lack of x, y or z, and that the answer must be to find *more of something good*. Driven by insecurity, we seek out better external conditions, attach to them, and inevitably suffer when the world ruthlessly takes them away from us.

By practicing mindfulness, we can reduce the portion of our conscious attention that is snatched away from us by the ego. As a result, our tendency to seek fulfilment by attaching to external conditions can be diminished.

The logic is simple: the more time we spend in a state of mindful awareness, rather than being lost in the comings and goings of the external, the more we're cementing our self-esteem onto more solid ground. As a result, we can gradually lose this underlying sense of insecurity, reducing our urge to crave constant improvements, as well as our tendency to get attached to external conditions.

By starting to pay attention to the comings and goings of the *inside* world in addition to the outside, we can start to watch this hopeless pursuit in action, and the belief that anything out there can hold the key is gradually revealed as a fallacy. Observe the mind intently and it becomes clear that happiness is something that comes from inside, not outside, and such that's where the work needs to be done.

It can be helpful to think of attachments as a burden on our backs that we're forced to carry around. Instead of spending our whole lives trying to perfect the exact components of this heavy load like we usually do, we can instead use mindfulness to start to offload it.

When these attachments are broken, they leave a space, which can generate a fresh feeling of insecurity or discontent. Left unchecked, the ego will go ahead and fill this space with something else – like going straight out to buy a puppy to forget all about the favourite shoes that we lost. We tend to go through life this way, with attachments coming and going like top-flight football managers, none of them achieving for us what they promised.

We usually spend all of our time juggling around the circumstances of our lives in order to find fulfilment, never appreciating the fact that we've got things to juggle in the first place. When we reduce our reliance on the existence of external conditions, we derive more of our self-esteem from just *being*, rather than placing so much on importance on being a certain way, or having a certain thing.

By cultivating mindfulness, the impact of the eternally discontent ego is reduced, and the compulsive need to attach to things will start to diminish. There is no additional step-by-step guide to follow here, since there is, pretty conveniently, only one step. Just use the techniques described to spend more time out of mind, and more time inside the space of pure awareness, and you'll encounter a far more profound and unwavering sense of 'you' than any combination of attachments could provide.

Why spend life looking to augment our identity with the external when, in reality, we're as complete as we're ever going to be? By practicing mindfulness, we can notice this fruitless game at play, and triumphantly declare that we're not playing any more.

Part 3: Real-Life Application

Now that we're fully briefed on some of the basic mechanisms of the ego, as well as what we've got in the toolbox, let's have a little drive around in our mindfulness van to see where we can put those tools to good use. In this section we'll be learning how to use the techniques of mindfulness to:

> Develop an inner state where the twists of fate no longer twist our nipples

> Keep a level head when everything starts going wrong

> Stand up for our opinions without being a dick about it

First, let's look at how we can reduce our super-tight attachment to the circumstances of our lives, uncovering a positive state of mind that's fortified against the ups and downs we experience along the way.

Singing In The Rain

I'm laughing at clouds,
So dark up above,
The sun's in my heart,
And I'm ready for love

Gene Kelly

One of the biggest attachments we cling to is to what's going on in our lives – the state of our career, relationships, finances, career relationships, finance careers, relationship finances, and so on. All together we can call this our 'life situation', or alternatively, how green the grass currently is on our side.

The more we derive our self-esteem from the current circumstances of our lives in this way, the more the ups and downs almost completely determine our state of mind at any given time. Although we'd love for things to be permanently great, we invariably vary between good or bad days, weeks, months and years. The inevitable result is a state of mind that's about as stable as a blob of lemon jelly on a unicycle.

The world is such a fickle pickle that even when things do happen to be playing out nicely, there's no guarantee that what we've got will be around for long: it's simply against the nature of the chaotic world we live in for things to stay just how we like them. For this reason, relying too heavily on the extent to which we're 'doing well' in order to feel content is always going to get us down in the end.

So your team won that big sports competition, you're the most popular guy on your floor of the office, and you wake up next to Miss Norwich every morning. This bundle of circumstances makes the ego feel really bloody good, so it attaches to them like there's no tomorrow.

Before you know it, your team has lost the next three big sports competitions, your desk has been moved up a floor next to IT (unlucky), and after you failed to reconcile reconcilable differences, your East Anglian honey has run off with Mr Felixstowe. Poor guy – everything that determined your happy state of mind has collapsed like a house of cards, leaving you collapsed unhappily in your house playing cards.

What's more, if the circumstances themselves don't eventually change, our feelings towards them probably will, and what makes us happy one day could make us miserable the next:

> You buy yourself an apple orchard, but after a few months come to realise that you actually prefer oranges
> You strive to find a partner to escape your lonely single existence, but fast forward a month and you're missing the fun of swiping through Tinder on the bus
> You dream for years of being an entrepreneur, but when you finally make it, you miss having time to flail aimlessly on

your oboe and watch a whole season of House of Cards in one day

Just when we've found peaches, we lust after plums, so happiness goes as soon as it comes. This occurs because of that *hedonic treadmill* we mentioned earlier: the satisfaction we gain from improving the external circumstances of our lives is very temporary and only exists because of the *contrast* to where we were before. When that contrast fades, so does the satisfaction, and at this point we'll start looking for ways to find the next hit.

Alan Watts raises the analogy of lying on a hard bed. We lie down on our right side, and it feels kinda comfy, because we've been standing up all day. However, after half an hour, we feel a little restless and find it agreeable to turn over. This new position feels great, but only in *contrast* to the last one, so when the contrast starts to fade, so does our satisfaction. In half an hour's time, the new position starts to get a little uncomfy, so we'd probably prefer to go back to the first. Buy a softer bed, and it'll solve the problem for a while, but only until the memory of the hard bed is lost – at which point some other problem will pop up to take its place. In sum: comfy only exists because of our experience of uncomfy, and it works the same way with striving for having a 'good' life situation. 'Doing well' is only a thing because '*not doing well*' is a thing, and the more we succeed in doing something, the greater will be the need to continue succeeding in order to remain content.

It looks like being overly attached to our life situation is bit of a nightmare – not only does the world unsympathetically wipe out circumstances that we like, but our greedy brains adjust very quickly to any 'improved' situation we manage to achieve.

For these reasons, having too much happiness riding on the extent to which we're doing well, or riding an *up*, isn't a great idea. Just like the other attachments we make, it only ends up causing unnecessary strife in the end. Fortunately, there's a much better way of going about things.

Mindfulness to the rescue

Look back over the past year and distinguish your high and low points – you might find that your state of mind quite reliably followed the ups and downs of your life's circumstances. When your relationships, careers, finances, finance career relationships (...you get the idea) were in a good state, so was your state of mind. This fluctuation reflects the tight attachment to our life situation.

When this attachment is strong, we start to crave the up cycles, and resist the downs. Considering that up only exists *because* of down, doing things in this way becomes like trying to keep both ends of a see-saw raised at all times. One side being high relies on the other being low, so we're inevitably going to be disappointed when it's impossible to maintain the high.

It thus becomes clear that it's not actually the absolute characteristics of what happens in our lives that determines our state of mind. In fact, the impact is almost entirely determined by our mental response: and it's lucky that that's the one out of the two that we can actually control. This is hugely empowering, and has the following implication: it's by no means necessary to limit feelings of content to when we're riding an up. Our capacity for mental acceptance can be slowly improved with practise, just like any other skill.

Simply spend more time practicing acceptance of the present moment, using meditation and day-to-day mindfulness, and this will train you to be more accepting of the circumstances of your life in general. The habit of fully accepting the present moment with mindfulness spreads into the acceptance of how our life situation is going, and the more this continues, the more that enjoyment of our current circumstances will override an obsession with snatching after the ups.

This doesn't mean running away from reality – it means creating an inner state where nothing external is able to upset the balance deep down. Mindfulness doesn't imply that we should strive to become like robots, unaffected by anything on the outside. Gaining an abundance of perspective on what ups and downs really are just means that we get affected by fluctuations in far healthier doses, and don't get shaken to the core when things aren't going how we'd hoped.

What's more, reducing our attachment to our life situation doesn't imply that there's no point in trying to improve our lives. Rather than losing the incentive to achieve anything, we're in fact in the best position to go for our goals when the fruits of our efforts – which are mostly chance anyway – no longer absolutely determine our state of mind:

> We still enjoy the ups, but we don't crave for them incessantly or cling to them when they come

> We still strive to improve our life situation, but we no longer foster any illusions about the extent to which achieving success is going to give us lasting happiness

> We still pursue our goals, but in total acceptance of however that pursuit decides to go, letting the fluctuations of the world help us along instead of fighting against them

So things aren't going so great – in a more mindful existence we just see what the low has in store, use it as an excuse to listen to our *'well sad'* playlist, and ride it out. It's about learning to appreciate each up and down for what it is, rather than demanding that every single period of our lives is a happy one (and sulking when it occasionally isn't). This is a strategy far more congruent with how things *actually* work, rather than how we wish they would.

Rather than toning down the celebration when our efforts do happen to pay off, with mindfulness comes the ability to treat the good for what it is, by throwing ourselves into it head first to enjoy the party while it lasts, without that element of loss when it inevitably passes. We can then go through life trying our best to improve our circumstances, occasionally succeeding but occasionally not, with our peace of mind intact the whole time. Sounds like a pretty sweet setup to me.

How To Not Fall Apart When Things Go A Bit Wrong

One of our mind's favourite things to do is to label everything – the people, situations, and events that we encounter. Putting things into mental boxes based on our existing preconceptions makes the world a lot less scary and a lot less confusing, and is an understandable result of an insecure ego. Not knowing anything about anything isn't exactly an appealing identity to attach to, so we label, judge, and feel better about ourselves as a result.

Evolutionarily speaking, it's no wonder that we developed this habit. Automatically labelling a famished lion springing towards us as dangerous, and initiating the appropriate adrenaline response to get some juice into our legs, was probably very useful in helping our ancestors achieve their understandable goal of *not becoming dead*.

Labelling and responding to things this way in the modern day, where we're at least 20 percent less likely to be attacked by lions, is not quite as essential. Regardless, the extremity of the reaction has lasted the generations, and our ancient fight-or-flight mechanism also shows up when we're late for work and can't find our keys. This fills us with adrenaline in a situation where we have no real use for it, also flooding our system with a load of other chemicals such as cortisol, the stress hormone.

As a result, it's much better to step back from these types of reactions in favour of a slightly more poised response – we can probably afford to take a little more time to assess a situation these days without getting a chunk bitten out of us (unless you happen to end up on a London night bus at 3am on a Saturday).

Not only do these reactive judgements fail to capture *part* of the truth, let alone the whole truth or nothing but the truth, but they can also cause us unnecessary suffering once we start resisting what we've determined as a negative situation. Once something is labelled as 'bad', it becomes a 'problem'. Our mental environment then descends into an orgy of negativity in order to work out why it happened, think of ways in which it could have been avoided, decide whose fault it was, and waste no time in mentally effing-and-jeffing at whoever we decided that to be.

Essentially, a whole lot of time and energy is put into resisting the situation that has arisen and simply wishing it wasn't so. These negative feelings can sometimes motivate us to make a change when one's possible, but they also tend to arise in situations where there's nothing we can do.

Let's say that we've missed the 33 bus by 33 seconds and we're going to be late for a job interview. The automatic reaction of intense frustration associated with watching that smug little bus drive off down the road is known to involve a tightening of the chest, an increased heart rate, and the sudden appearance of fifty shades of red in the facial complexion.

These reactions are a result of an instinctive resistance to the way that life turned out that morning – or more accurately, the way it didn't turn out (the way that we'd planned). This stems from the human tendency to create an idyllic 'story' in our heads for how we'd like things to go, and attaching to it.

Being attached to things going a certain way in a world that rarely caters to our wants is inevitably going to cause us to suffer. In this case, we got attached to all of the following things occurring: waking up on time, catching the bus, performing well in the interview, being offered the job. When anything comes along to disrupt this course of events, like missing the bus, a huge about of resistance is generated. We simply don't want to be in the situation that we find yourself in, since we're attached to a different one. We've judged the present situation as bad, and want to be on that bus, not where we are, crying into our prep notes at the bus stop.

The strange assumption in this case is that tossing and turning and wheezing and moaning and booing and crying and whatnot will somehow bring us back to the fairytale sequence of events we'd attached to. Fight, fight and fight some more in our minds against what's happening (and everything that's led up to it), but in the end it will all be to no avail.

We may be perfectly in the right to be cursing our luck – or cursing the fact that we decided to spend an extra ten minutes conditioning our hair because Cosmo said it would help our application along – but such an emotional reaction to situations going sour is unhelpful and unnecessary.

Crying over spilt milk is our natural setting, and we will continue to cry over this milk until we reprogram ourselves to dustpan-and-brush it back into the bottle and have a delicious glass anyway (...3 second rule).

Who you gonna call? Hint: begins with 'm'

Our reaction to adversity does *not* have to be adoption of the mental foetal position. By being more mindful, we can start to undo our usual habit patterns, and stop ourselves from reacting to perceived adversity by shooting ourselves in the foot with bullets of needless resistance.

If you ever notice that the situation you find yourself in is making you suffer, for any reason at all, remember that it's always in your power to take a step back behind the waterfall. The state of awareness is a place that's unaffected by that which it's aware of, in the same way that a mirror isn't affected by what it reflects. The anxiety we experience during adversity is just another *content* of our awareness, so it's always possible to take a step back from it. This is incredibly empowering: as long as we're rooted in awareness itself, neither the situation nor the anxiety has the ability to bring us down.

A great illustration of detachment from our instinctive reaction to a situation is to think about what it's like when we're are giving other people advice about *their* problems, explained succinctly by Ryan Holiday in 'The Obstacle Is The Way':

What happens when we give people advice? Their problems are crystal clear to us, the solutions obvious. Something that's present when we deal with our own obstacles is always missing when we hear other people's problems: the baggage. With other people we can be objective. We take the situation at face value and immediately set about helping our friend to solve it. Selfishly – and stupidly – we save the pity and the sense of persecution and the complaints for our own lives.

Mindfulness is a great practical solution for achieving this baggage-free perspective on our own problems, as soon as they start to make as suffer. By observing our initial judgements and emotional reactions from a place of awareness, we can reduce our tendency to let them dictate our state of mind. Remember: just as we are not our thoughts, we aren't our negative reactions either. They are just a by-product of a mind that habitually resists the negative with no useful consequences at all, so if a judgement arises that isn't helpful, it's our choice to let it float on outta there.

When you think about it, the judgement of something as a 'problem' is linked to the amount of resistance that arises, but not to the mind's actual ability to solve it. Rather than wasting energy on pointlessly wishing whatever it was wasn't so, once we fully come to terms with a situation, the mind can be fully put to work on finding a solution if possible (or just accepting fate if not). It doesn't matter what we should have done, or how we wished things would have turned out – it's a lot more useful to be concerned with what we *can* do, with what's actually happening.

When we cultivate mindfulness, this starts to become our default response to adversity – focusing on the raw facts of the present moment and acting rationally from there. I can't tell you that this'll make the bus that you missed turn around and pick you up, but it'll put you in a clear and balanced state of mind, one that'll be far more effective for getting to grips with what needs to be done. Mindfulness helps you to let go of your idea of what you wanted to happen as soon as it doesn't happen, so that you can start to focus on what's still possible: catching the next bus, hailing a cab, or starting to walk.

Try getting into the habit of responding to adversity by taking five long, deep breaths, and focusing on every aspect of the breathing process as you do it. Even this short exercise, which takes no time at all, will be enough to root you in the present and help you to respond, rather than react, to whatever's happening.

When it comes down to it, we can either choose to be in sync with life by welcoming its curveballs, or resist it by running away from them. Doing the former isn't always easy, but the more you practise mindfulness, the easier it will become to return to equilibrium whenever a difficult situation chucks you away from it. Rather than habitually resisting what life throws your way, you'll start to chuckle light-heartedly at your mind whenever it starts making a big deal out of bit of adversity.

This is definitely one of the biggest differences that mindfulness can make to our day-to-day existence. When we start just *going with* whatever circumstances we're handed with no resistance or emotional reaction, we're stepping out of battles that there's no point in fighting, and conserving our energy for the ones we can win.

How To Have Opinions Without Being a Dick About It

Being attached to our opinions is a great opportunity for the ego to try and achieve one of its favourite goals: being right. For this reason, we're incredibly fond of trusting our judgements and opinions with great loyalty, and rising up to defend them when they're challenged. In reality it's incredibly optimistic to think that what we think now is what we'll still think in five years' time, let alone something that's nearing the truth.

We have such a strong bias for the unique basket of experiences and information that have influenced us that we attach ourselves to our opinions and defend them as though they could be objectively superior to anybody else's. This leads to a load of unnecessary judgements, arguments, and a load of other no-no's that make the ego feel better but the *world feel worse.*

Suppose Harriet is a bit of a health nut, so she feels pretty disgusted when she sees someone lighting up a E-Cigarette nearby. Harriet walks past, *tut-tut-tut*s, and tells him that he should get rid of that futuristic cancer stick before *it* gets rid of *him* – an objection that seems fair enough, since smoking is really, really, really bad for you.

However, to force her judgement on someone in this way ignores the possibility that others may hold a wildly different view of the world than she does. What if smokey Sam lives by the philosophy that life is short anyway, so believes it makes sense to just do what he feels like while he's around? He's perfectly aware that his E-ciggy is bad for him, but at this point in time with his current philosophy on life, he doesn't really care that much.

For whatever reason, Sam puts a higher value on living fast and dying young while Harriet puts a higher value on healthy living. Which side you take in the matter as you're reading this is largely irrelevant – making a judgement like Harriet's is an attempt to enforce her values on someone else (under the assumption that hers are better), and reflects her assumption that the high value she places on health is the *right* way. *Tut-tut-tut* right back, Harriet[1].

Since pretty much all of our opinions are formed by some form of value judgement or other, we can never, ever, ever see them as objectively superior to anybody else's. This doesn't mean that we shouldn't have opinions – it just means that it's always best to remember that subjective judgements of value is all that they are, so they shouldn't be forced on others.

The passionate support we devote to our own points of view stems from the fact that we've attached to them – likely for

---

[1] Tut-tut-tut right back at me, then, I guess, for making the judgement that Harriet shouldn't make judgements.

the motive of fortifying our self-image of someone who knows a lot about the world. Just like with all of our other attachments, holding on tight to our beliefs can cause great suffering when something, or someone, comes along to challenge them.

Arguments are a great way to illustrate just how defensive the ego can get when the beliefs that form its identity are challenged. Let's say that you've found yourself in an argument about which is closer – the Sun or the Moon. Your mates are adamant that the Sun is closer, whereas you're trying to convince them otherwise. Suppose that they won't back down, telling you that that guy down the pub, who is so smart that he almost always gets his pound back (at least) at the Pub Quiz machine, told them that it was so, and as such, it must be so.

Cast your mind back to the last time you were involved in a similar situation, and try and remember how it felt. Frustrating, right? When we gain some of our identity from our opinions, even the knowledge of someone else floating through life ignorant of what we'd consider a basic truth can be incredibly infuriating – but when they're spouting (what we perceive as) their ignorance all over the room during an argument, it's even worse. It's as though we become the sole spokesperson for the side who is 'right' and feel like we have a duty to convince the other side otherwise. We feel the need to reap the win that we know we deserve.

This is simply the ego in action. It's become so identified with its side of the argument that even the existence of a contrary point of view is enough to dig its ribs. If you think about it, there is no rational reason for that attachment. You may end up being right, but the truth (whatever it is) is unaffected by whether you believe in it or not – the Sun and the Moon are entirely indifferent to your passionate support, and they're going to get on with business as usual up there regardless. Whether you convince someone of something or not doesn't make a difference to anything except the satisfaction of the ego.

If we have a big emotional reaction when one of our opinions or beliefs is suddenly called into question, it's because what we're defending is built on dodgy foundations – in other words, our attachment to believing the belief is probably stronger than our actual belief of the belief. When someone presents us with information that seems to contradict what we think, it shouldn't cause a negative reaction unless we are overly motivated by maintaining our attachments (by agreeing with our past self) than by potentially learning from others' point of view.

Of course, this doesn't imply that we shouldn't try and grasp as much of the truth as we can. It just means that we should realise that in the grand scheme of things we understand dick all, so there's no point wasting too much time or effort defending ourselves or trying to convince others – it's a game with no winner.

Mindfulness saves the day

Going through life attached to our beliefs and opinions is only going to cause drama and suffering, because opinions are like arseholes: everybody's got one, and being too identified with yours is fairly unhealthy. Fortunately, it doesn't have to be this way.

By practicing mindfulness, we're less likely to seek security by attaching to opinions, and more able to take a step back when we get drawn into aggressively defending these opinions. In a more mindful existence, nothing that we derive our identity from runs the risk of being challenged by debates and disagreements, so they're far less likely to spiral into shouting matches.

When proving to everybody just how right we are is no longer driving us, *'you know what, let's forget it and go for an ice cream'* is recognised as an infinitely better outcome than either winning an argument (and the hardening of our attachment to *being right*) or losing it (being shaken to the core and sulking in a corner somewhere).

We all know that feeling when someone attacks something we believe in, or makes a firm statement that we believe to be false. However much truth the antagonist's statement may hold, if it's against something we're attached to, the alarm bells sound and we rise up to defend it, full of emotion.

By just taking five deep breaths and heading into the present to watch that blood rush up to the head, waiting a while for it to swirl around and trickle back down – congrats! You've started to form that all-important gap between you and the attachment. You'll be able to *respond*, not *react*, to whatever or whoever is challenging you. Keep practicing mindfulness and no one will be able to push your buttons in this way. In fact, you won't even *have* buttons anymore.

This doesn't mean that in a more mindful life you never assert yourself in discussions. You can still say 'I massively, massively disagree with everything you've just said', but whether you convince anybody of your point of view no longer matters so much to you anymore, since the attachment to opinions isn't as strong. If we don't derive any sort of identity from 'being on the right side', whether anyone listens to or believes what we were standing for doesn't make a lick of difference to our peace of mind.

In a more mindful existence, we cease to rely on such attachments to make us feel secure. This way, we can have a perfectly nice time believing what we want to believe, and standing up for it, without simultaneously feeling our claws coming out and our world crashing down if somebody hints that they might not agree.

Part 4: Why Can't We Be Friends? The Practical Benefits of Mindfulness

As we've seen, overly relying on the outside world to find happiness is a losing game that doesn't have much chance of satisfying us in the long run. However, as long as we keep this in mind, there's no harm in looking at some of the ways that cultivating a more mindful state can help us level up. Since mindfulness is currently being used all over the world in the name of productivity, it would be a shame not to at least touch base (this is a modern book for modern people, after all).

Using awareness and thought as a dynamic duo can give a much welcome boost to a load of practical pursuits, which we'll look at in this chapter. The only sticking point is that seeing mindfulness as a productivity tool can be a bit of a bastardisation of what is a deeply profound technique – but don't worry, I'll steer you away from any pitfalls.

In this chapter, we're going to have a look at:

> How mindfulness can give the thinking mind a bubble bath when it's knackered

> How to give a mindful boost to problem-solving and the creativity process

> Using the insight gained from self-observation to nudge the practical aspects of life into a better direction for us

In defence of the thinking mind

As you may have noticed, the thinking mind has taken quite a battering in this book so far, but it would be wrong to give the impression that thinking is always harmful, and that the only worthwhile goal is pure awareness without thought[1].

In fact, thinking is *fantastic*. The mind is an incredibly powerful tool, a fact that speaks for itself when looking at the phenomenal feats of human accomplishment even in the last decade or so (landing a spacecraft on a moving comet, finding the Higgs-boson particle, inventing the spork). The brain's ability to get stuck into whatever problems it's been given is something truly magnificent, and the suffering it causes is only an innocent by-product of trying its best to make sense of all the info we cram into it.

Unfortunately, the sheer amount of juicy information that's available for the mind to sink its teeth into these days – most of which is of little absolute importance – has led to it firing

[1] If any Zen masters are reading and disagree with this notion, I'm glad to discuss it over brunch in your tea-house up Mount Fuji, if you'll have me.

on all cylinders at pretty much all times. If you know guns, which I don't, you'll know that if we don't prevent some of these cylinders from firing at least some of the time, there might be an explosion, or something, maybe.

Mindfulness does not go so far as to discourage the use of the thinking mind for practical purposes, since modern life will inevitably be full of problems to solve, appointments to rearrange, and outfits to plan. Instead, a more mindful life makes it easier to take a step back from this mental activity when we fancy it, something that not only improves peace of mind for us, but also improves the functioning of the mind itself.

A better way

The thinking mind is a genius, but as is the case with most geniuses, a sacrifice of sanity has been made somewhere along the way. This shows in the mind's habit of making life way more difficult for us than it needs to be.

However, it isn't thought itself that's the problem, but our *identification* with it that we need to be concerned with. Therefore, getting rid of thought altogether is not our aim here – so finding a better balance between the default mode of operation, known as 'gung ho!', and the more peaceful standby mode of awareness, is the goal. This will go a good way towards toning down this insanity, leaving the genius part untouched and free to help us out.

The mind loves having things to work out, but its horsepower is diminished by an incessant hyperactivity that restricts it from doing its problem-solving thing. Minimise this impact with mindfulness and we can witness the mind operating as a well-oiled machine instead of a preoccupied, spluttering mess.

Let's look at some examples of how using mindfulness to occasionally step out of the world of thoughts, things, and thoughts about things actually makes us *better* at navigating and mastering that world.

Productivity and problem-solving

If you're working on a project, or even have a big decision to make, think about it a whole lot, then just sit and meditate... When you quieten your mind down, you allow your subconscious to mull over what you've given it, without overstuffing it. This is when those 'eureka' moments can happen.

Steve Jobs

Just think about it deeply, then forget it... an idea will jump up in your face.

Don Draper off Mad Men

One way in which decreasing our reliance on conscious thought can help us out is when we're stuck with a vague or difficult problem to solve, choice to make, or situation to deal with. It's often the case that even signing up every last brain cell for the task won't get us to anything conclusive – this is because while some problems can be figured out fairly quickly by the conscious mind (*what's the square root of 25?*), ambiguous ones often can't be solved straight away by just thinking really hard.

As our man Don Draper suggested back in the fictional fifties or sixties or something, whenever we're faced with a difficult problem it's often a good strategy to think about it as much as humanly possible, and then just forget all about it until something pops up.

In fact, most theories of creativity grant a role to some form of 'incubation' in the creative process[1], so I'm pretty sure this is what Don was getting at. This means that once all of the relevant information has been soaked up by the conscious mind, it starts to trickle downward to the subconscious, where it starts to organically rearrange itself into a better formation – like when you start off solving a jigsaw by getting all the edge pieces in place.

[1] Most notably Graham Wallas' 1926 model, which Wikipedia tells me is the most famous and time-tested theory on how creativity functions (although it's possible Graham added that part in himself)

Maybe Don was right. By continuing to work flat out on a difficult problem, only enlisting the help of the conscious mind, we're preventing the optimal functioning of this cog in the creativity machine – the part that'll probably end up solving it in the end. Just *not thinking* about whatever it is for a bit is enough to set this process in motion, but why stop there – how about toning down conscious thought altogether? This helps in the same way as *sleeping on it* does – give the conscious mind a break when it's wheezing and puffing, and the subconscious will be ready to come off the bench.

Next time you're stuck on a problem and are in need of a boost (or just have a mountain of work to do) give the process a mindful cutting edge. Any method of getting yourself into the present will help, but here's three specific ways you could do it:

1) Instead of going full-throttle, try alternating focused work (25 mins) with breath meditation (5 mins) – this creates a mental environment much more conducive to staying focused and avoiding fatigue during a long day (a conclusion supported by the men in white coats, who have shown that mindfulness can have significant positive effects on concentration, alertness, and creative problem-solving[ix]).

2) If the problem's a biggie, like an important life decision, push yourself to the very limit of conscious thought by

writing a breakdown of your problem down clearly, getting down every single piece of relevant information. After that, nip off to meditate for a bit. When the timer's up and you go back to that breakdown and read over it, there's no doubt you'll have a better grasp of the solution than before (or at least get a feeling for a rough direction).

3) When you take your lunch break from working on a tough problem or project, don't instinctively get on Facebook, check your emails, and devour 10 online articles – give your brain a break! After you've bought your lunch, sit down somewhere nice, and just *eat your sandwich*. Forget everything else, and just *eat*. Be aware of your sensations, internal narration, mastication duration, and saliva creation with a patient, mindful meditation that'll provide inflation to your appreciation of the starvation termination situation.

...just make sure you've got something to write on, because practicing mindfulness while your subconscious is churning through a problem is the perfect environment for the arising of new insights. By creating some space in your conscious attention, those all-important fresh insights will have an easier time floating up from below. You'll return to your project not only with a well-rested mind, but more than likely a notepad full of ideas that popped up because you gave them a chance to.

Thinking and awareness, when used together in tandem in this way, hold the power to help unlock whatever difficult situation or problem that we throw at them – or they'll at least help us feel out the next step in its solution if it's a toughy.

Intuition

As well as helping us tackle problems effectively by giving the thinking mind a rest, mindfulness also brings a load of benefits that stem from increasing our self-awareness.

For example, it can help us tap into the kind of intuition that doesn't show itself via the thinking mind – that compass inside us that's pointing towards what we really want, rather than what we think we want[1]. These feelings don't come up as a thoughts, so they can't really be put into words – browsing the dessert menu, what do we use to decide between the chocolate brownie and the banana split? Scrolling through our iPod, what is it that makes us land on a particular artist?

It's not the thinking mind that helps us out in these situations – the insight is coming from somewhere outside the chaos of conscious thought. We're not exactly sure *why* we fancy listening to Barry Manilow's entire back catalogue this

[1] Credit to Marianne Cantwell's excellent 'Be A Free Range Human' for a good discussion of this compass, or, the 'internal GPS'.

afternoon, but we just *want to*. Rather than just a comment from our inner monologue, it's more like an internal compass deeper down, trying to point us in the right direction – one that we usually can't pay attention to under all the noise. Yep, you guessed it – mindfulness can help us out with this one.

Whenever you're mulling over a life decision (or a dessert decision), try taking your attention inward and staying there for a while, as you think about each option in turn. Put all your attention on the sensations that arise – changes in emotion, heart rate, or tightening of the chest. The idea is that when something's in tune with your gut feelings, the resulting '*ding ding ding*!' always manifests in some kind of sensation or other – so if we take our attention inside, we can start to try and pin-point it.

For example, you may notice a certain approval, enthusiasm or lightness come about when thinking about some options, whereas others may bring with them a sort of heavy 'aw, shucks...' feeling. You might also feel that one option has a sort of 'pull' to it, whereas the other ticks lots of logical boxes, but doesn't get you excited deep down. Try and get well acquainted with the difference of sensation between the two – and try to pin down and really analyse every aspect of the first one. This is the one you should probably start looking for each time you've got a decision to make.

The idea of following this internal compass may seem a little idealistic – obviously the idea of taking a 6 month holiday will more likely arouse this deep-down sense of approval than the idea of 6 months double shifts – but it's still useful to become more aware of whether our actions and decisions are in tune with our wants or not. Actually figuring out the logistics, once we know what's right for us, is the point where we call the thinking mind back in from the waiting room to do its job.

By getting in touch with our intuition in this way, we slowly reduce the impact of ego's various agendas on our decision making – making this one of the biggest practical benefits to be gained from cultivating mindfulness.

Being on top form

A similar benefit of a more mindful life is that when we're more observant of our behaviour, we can start to take note of the times where we're bouncing off the walls with enthusiasm, and compare them with the times where we retreat into our shell – sort of like using the *inner compass* to work out whether a particular environment is good for us or not.

Think back to the last time that you were, as your friends might describe, on 'top form'. You were feeling confident, enthusiastic, and were generally having a better time of it, whatever 'it' was at the time. Similarly, try and recall the last time you were in a situation that made you quiet, reserved, and not feel like yourself.

Compare the two – where were you, and what were you doing? Were you just with friends or family, or were you surrounded by a load of new people? By reflecting on which types of situations tend to make you feel a certain way, you're in a better position to pinpoint situations that make you shine, and then make a conscious choice to increase how frequently you find yourself in them.

For example, they say that we're hugely influenced by the five people that we spend the most time with, and whoever they are that say that, I'm with them. Think briefly about the people in your life that are energy-givers: full of enthusiasm, fresh ideas and optimism, and when you're with them, you really feel like yourself. Next, think about the ones that are energy-sappers: often complaining, shooting things down, and when they're around, you feel inhibited about being yourself at all. Life's too short to spend more time feeling restrained or unworthy than is absolutely unnecessary, so upon reflection you might find that you're spending too much time with the sappers, and not enough with the givers.

Of course, we shouldn't see a situation in which the company we are keeping is less-than-ideal as a sort of obstacle to be overcome – it's always good to practise mindful acceptance when we're feeling a little uncomfortable. However, full acceptance of these situations doesn't imply that we can't take steps to find ourselves in them less often in the long run. We often tend to forget that we pretty much have complete control over what we spend our time doing, and who we spend our time doing those things with – and as such, there's always potential to nudge things into a better direction for us.

Everybody, including you, likes you more when you're at your best. Use a bit of mindful self-observation to notice the circumstances that fill you with life, and you can start to fill your life with times where you're full with life.

Career choices

Observing your reactions and behaviour more attentively can give you a massively useful helping hand in the practical world when it comes to thinking about possible career moves. Discover that you're in fact a dodecahedron, and you'll realise that continuing to force yourself into a round hole for half of your waking life is never going to be that rewarding.

The thing about genuine talents is that they're often difficult to spot because they come to us so naturally – what would require significant effort for someone else happens to flow through us with ease, so the biggest thing we have to offer could be hiding right under our nose. By taking our attention inside, it's easier to notice what really pushes our buttons, and what un-pushes them. What floats our boat, and what sinks it. What tickles our pickle, and what throws it in the bin. This can help us start to realise where our likes, dislikes, strengths and weaknesses are, and once we've got a firm grip on this, it can get us started on working out a tailor-made direction to head in.

Have a think about it now to get a taste – when was the last time you spent hours and hours on a project or task, and the time just flew? What types of things do you always seem to notice faults with, that other people don't? When you're more aware of your reactions to situations in your working life, you'll start to notice which types of tasks, projects and hobbies really make you feel alive, and which make your heart sink.

This is where you can start to exploit your real value, rather than forcing yourself into some other mould or box out of convenience or apathy – it's no grand claim that things will generally tend to go better for you when you start to take advantage of your natural talents. Of course, this doesn't mean that you should quit your job because you've worked out you're really good at 17th century erotic playwriting – it just means that it can be hugely insightful to place more attention on what unique contribution you can make to the world. It's always possible to pay more attention to the parts of your existing role that you love, and those which you hate, and formulate the changes from there.

They say a man who loves his job never works a day in his life, and whoever they are, I'm with them, too. The more your career taps into your genuine strengths and natural motivations, the more it will cease to become work – once you find your niche, other people will be amazed at how you manage to float through life so easily.

The Middle Way

Throughout the last section we've been learning how to combine mindfulness with thought to improve some of the practical aspects of our lives. This is an understandable to-do to-do: there's a world out there, and it would be a shame not to fully explore the possibilities, and see how far we can go. Unfortunately, we get so hypnotised by the world *out* there that we forget all about the world *in* there – and though there's nothing inherently wrong with improving our life situation, it regularly makes us miserable simply because *we're doing it wrong.*

Our complete identification with the ego, which has a pretty nasty seeking habit, causes us to reduce our interaction with the outside world into an exercise from which there should always something to be *gained* in some way. The problem is that the world is entirely indifferent to this agenda, so we're regularly disappointed when our strict criteria for contentment aren't fulfilled. Which, depending on how often we have our ego-tinted glasses on, can happen hundreds of times a day.

As we've seen throughout this book, taking our attention inside is enough to reveal that happiness stems from our *reaction* to the circumstances of our lives, rather than just the circumstances themselves – so it follows that to get any real insight into the process, we have to stop ourselves from focusing exclusively on the latter. It's not particularly complicated to start doing this – all we have to do is spend less time lost in thought, and more time using present moment awareness to step behind the waterfall and watch it all go down. Use mindfulness to get in touch with the part of us that doesn't come and go, and we lose the need to try and extract happiness from the things that do – so the endless seeking of the ego is suppressed.

However, there may seem to be one part missing: if our constant 'seeking' never ends up satisfying us, are we supposed to sever all our ties with the outside world, move to the jungle, make like an ape-man and just sit there being aware of the trees?

This is an understandable question, and it has a simple answer: yes. Striving to achieve in a world such as this one is only going to make us miserable, so there's no point in even trying. I know a pretty nice spot in Sumatra if you fancy joining – we'll sit in the trees and eat bananas all day, just like an ape-man.

Just kidding (as great as that sounds). In fact, it's entirely possible to reconcile a mindful life with one where we strive to achieve great things. The alternative to mindless craving does not have to be passive apathy, and the understanding that many things are out of our control does not have to stop us from influencing the things that are.

There's a middle way, and this is it: *still going for it, but not being attached to the results* – or put another way, trying our best, but not deriving our self-esteem from the extent to which we succeed. Non-attachment to the fruits of our labour hits the sweet spot between contentment and achievement, and gives us freedom to strive for 'good' conditions, while discouraging us from having too much riding on it. This way, the comings and goings and ups and downs and lefts and rights of our lives then cease to be able to shake us to the core in the way that they used to.

This may seem like it would sap the incentive out of achievement, but it doesn't. When you think about it, what's normally motivating us to achieve is an underlying feeling of 'not enough', of 'I need to become this, and then I'll be happy'. By using mindfulness to nudge us towards this middle way, our motivating force becomes the joy of the path itself, and it's not difficult to see how this is going to end up better in the long run. Head back out into the world of things with peace of mind established as a primary, and pursuit of the secondary – goals, achievements, and *goin' for stuff* – becomes a lot less serious, a lot more effective, and a lot more fun.

For example, when we try our best to succeed without the obsessive attachment to the outcome, the idea of failure becomes a lot less scary, so we're encouraged to be even braver with what we attempt. What's more, by learning to fully accept fate when we're faced with a failure of some kind, without for a second wishing things had turned out differently, we have the best opportunity to take effective action from wherever 'trying our best' left us (even if it wasn't very far). Our capacity for achievement will undoubtedly increase this way, since we're no longer fighting *against* anything – whatever happens is cool with us.

For these reasons, switching lanes towards the *middle way* between contentment and achievement will always deliver the best results in the end – get the inside right, and the outside will follow. By improving our ability not to cling so tightly to our pre-conceived ideas about how we wanted everything to turn out, we're in a better position to realise when life was actually lending a helping hand, when it seemed like it was trying to flick us in the parts.

When there's no longer any possible circumstance that could come along and wipe out everything our identity depended on, whether we're riding an up or a down doesn't affect us so deeply anymore. This doesn't mean we don't enjoy the ups, and don't ever get down about the downs. We just heed the words of avant-garde philosopher Ronan Keating by learning to appreciate that life will inevitably be a very, very, very bumpy rollercoaster ride – so there's no real choice but to ride it.

By getting more in touch with that which doesn't leave us – awareness itself – we can start to use it as a loyal seatbelt throughout this ride, which stays intact throughout the whole shebang. When life's bumps lose their power to throw us headfirst out of the carriage, we're free to scream, wave, laugh, cry, pee our pants, whatever – and simply enjoy each up and down as it comes with peace of mind intact.

The bumps are what make the whole thing so damn enjoyable, after all. So stop worrying, strap on your seatbelt, smile for the photo, and putcha arms in the air like you *just don't care.*

Conclusion

"I can show you,
That when it rains or shines,
It's just a state of mind"

The Beatles, *'Rain'*

Me and you have been on a journey for the last hundred pages or so – a journey not unlike life itself. There have been ups, downs, laughs, frowns, illusions revealed and truth-oranges peeled. But remember, they were all just temporary fluctuations, so it's best not to get too attached. That's behind us now, and it's time to see where this all leaves us.

As we've seen, taking a mindful look inward is a fascinating exploration that slowly reveals that an awful lot of the suffering we experience is self-created, and an inevitable result of the way our mind works by default. Although happiness is something that we all desire, we grasp for it with wildly differing levels of competency, and wildly differing levels of success. As it stands, many of us find ourselves lost in a game that's about as winnable as playing *you're-it* with a bumblebee.

It's clear that how good things look on paper isn't what matters for happiness – so an inquiry into what does matter seems profoundly worthwhile. There's one thing we know for sure: our minds aren't exactly doing a stellar job of handling this inquiry so far. While some people are getting by just fine, for others, it's a drag – and the side we fall on has nothing to do with how our life looks from the outside.

This suffering stems from a default mode of operation that, fortunately for us, our main man Buddha figured out is not the only way to be. He discovered that the only way of seeing things how they really are is to examine that which is unspoiled by concepts, judgements, good, or bad – consciousness itself. Props due to the guy – he was really onto something. By observing the mind from the *safe zone* of pure awareness, the habit patterns that negate our best efforts for happiness are revealed as just that – deep-rooted, conditioned habits, and ones that are within our power to change.

It therefore looks like what we're seeking might not be quite as elusive as we might have thought. Most of us never realise this, and live as though it's not possible to be happy *before* all of our numerous desires are satisfied, *before* our various goals are achieved. In fact, as people all over the world have been discovering for thousands of years, it is in fact entirely possible to just *be* happy, rather than needing to *become* happy. The problem's been that Buddhists have never felt the need to shout their discoveries from the rooftops – they're content just to meditate quietly on their rooftops instead, so news hasn't exactly spread quickly.

This isn't the only reason that taking an inward turn hasn't has been a pursuit that many of us have taken up. A big problem with making any kind of entry into the so-called 'spiritual' world is that, being honest with you, it's an absolute minefield out there. Take one wrong step and you get blown to pseudoscientific oblivion, and you'll be unlikely to fancy dipping your toe in again anytime soon.

To illustrate: the first result in Amazon's 'Religion & Spirituality' section is self-help phenomenon 'The Secret', a book that uses *quantum physics* to explain that all you need to do to achieve what you want in life (like winning the lottery, or curing your cancer) is to visualise your desires obsessively, and as long as you think hard enough, the universe will deliver. By the way, this also extends to not looking at fat people if you want to lose weight, and proposes that natural disasters, unspeakable war crimes, and terminal illnesses tend to strike those who *just weren't thinking in the right way*. It's doesn't take a lifetime of meditation to figure out why that whole section of the bookshop has a bad rep.

Unfortunately, the bad apples seem to spoil the bunch, and the understandable reaction is to tar anything 'spiritual' with the 'not-for-me' brush. While we would all agree that it makes sense to learn more about our minds, as soon as the word 'spiritual' gets attached, we make like a shepherd, and get the flock outta there.

However, unlike some other viewpoints you'll encounter, mindfulness' answer to this natural human curiosity is not an extravagant one: simply take a closer look at the reality of the mind, and a couple of pretty interesting things start to become clear. This isn't a wild claim, and there's no need to take anybody's word for anything – the benefits of mindfulness can be discovered in the personal laboratory of your own mind.

What's more, it's increasingly possible to test these claims in *actual* science labs. Although the pseudo-scientific baggage of the past hasn't done much to help mindfulness' appeal to the cynics, modern studies – with far more rigorous experimental standards, conducted by scientists whose degrees didn't come off the internet – are starting to build momentum. What's more, thanks to rapid developments in technology, many of the barriers that have restricted effective research into mindfulness in the past are being lifted.

Most exciting for us in the mindfulness game are the developments in the neuroscience game – particularly the recent discovery of *neuroplasticity*, which refuted the long-held belief that the brain stops changing after a certain age, instead proving the ability of the brain to change its structure depending on what it experiences. This discovery has some pretty gnarly implications – most notably that if the brain adapts to what it experiences, it figures that we could use specific techniques to provide our brains the experiences necessary to change them in the ways that we'd like, just like we work out different areas of our body with different exercise routines.

The rousing conclusion from these developments is as simple as it is profound, and something that goes against many of the assumptions of the Western culture: *happiness is a skill.* It's not this mysterious, elusive holy grail, that we might get as long as everything pans out well for us – it's something that's generated by the brain, and now that we know that our brains are trainable, it follows that lasting happiness is up for grabs by anyone who puts in those gym-hours. This a conclusion that's only just starting to make waves in the scientific world, and seeing as though achieving happiness is pretty much the sole aim of our lives, it's a conclusion with deeply profound implications.

Not that they would ever be *those guys*, but in regard to these discoveries, the Buddhists would hate to say they told us so. There have been millions of practitioners throughout the ages who've been well aware that the default mode of operation up there in the wrinkly pink is one that's within our power to change – people have been using mindfulness meditation as a methodical practice to greatly improve their states of consciousness and end their day-to-day suffering for literally thousands of years.

This doesn't make the recent findings of neuroscience any less valuable, however. Our increasing ability to correlate human experiences of changing consciousness with corresponding physical changes in the brain is a hugely exciting development, and having a look at which specific areas of the brain are affected by techniques like meditation is a fascinating avenue that the scientific community is eagerly starting to explore. The study of the effects of various types of meditation on the brain is becoming a little more like our study of bodily exercise, which opens the doors to some ridiculously interesting avenues:

> What's the minimum amount of practice necessary to experience noticeable benefits from meditation? Is there a maximum level, past which we don't get any more benefit?
> Which areas of the brain change while we are meditating, and how long does it take for them to go back to normal? Is it possible to make lasting changes to these areas?
> How do different types of meditation affect the brain differently? What's the best type for reducing stress, which is best for increasing concentration, and most importantly, which is best for facilitating happiness?

In fact, the men in white coats have already started having a go at answering some of these questions – and they're showing that we have more power to change our minds than we realised. A review of the recent literature reveals that not only has mindfulness practice been shown to improve cognitive skills like concentration, problem-solving and emotional regulation[iv] while reducing anxiety, pain, and depression[v]. but it's even been shown to work out certain

125

parts of the brain and make them *bigger*. Studies have shown meditation to increase grey matter thickness in a number of regions, such as the ones associated with self-awareness, compassion, learning, memory, and emotional regulation[vi]. If I say so myself, which I do, beefing up our brains isn't a bad return on an investment of having a little sit down for twenty minutes per day.

It's undeniable that the world of mindfulness and meditation is headed in a pretty awesome direction – one of peer-reviewed scientific inquiry, trial and error, and tangible results – and if research continues to show benefits on such a wide scale, the mindfulness 'fad' isn't going to go anywhere anytime soon. Of course, until the body of research thickens up a bit, it's not cool to be making any huge claims, or all the hard work done to improve meditation's chronic PR problem will be reversed. However, when research is starting to hint that a simple, accessible and most importantly *free* technique could have such far-reaching benefits, there's only so long we can ignore it.

It's becoming obvious that there's a compromise to be struck between an oversensitive bullshit detector and blind devotion, between unwavering cynicism and unwavering faith. This compromise is found in the growing numbers that are starting to begin an investigation of their inner worlds, but with their welly boots of scepticism strapped on tight – making sure to avoid wrong turns, but encouraged to continue because the occasional glimpses of what can be found further along are just too profound to ignore.

These people are not wearing robes and gowns, but business suits, chefs hats, hospital scrubs and army uniforms. There are millions of these people around, and as we enter an age where scientific enquiry, rationality and free-thinking continues to eclipse the impact of age-old dogma, they're increasingly starting to come out of the woodwork.

People are increasingly finding out for themselves just how much we have to gain from *changing our minds,* and you could be one of them – the ball is in your court. Happiness isn't waiting for us somewhere out there – it's something we decide for ourselves. All we've got to do is follow the instructions (you can find simple ones in the back), and it's ours.

We tend to pursue happiness like it's a pair of lost sunglasses. We rack our brains, empty out our drawers, and buy books called '*find your sunglasses in 30 days, guaranteed!*' – then when it doesn't work, we still believe it's because we just aren't looking hard enough.

You know what? They were sitting on our heads all along.

Happiness is right where we left it. Have a look in the other direction, and you'll see.

Next steps

First of all, thanks for reading! I hope you enjoyed yourself, I know I did!

Second of all, if you had as agreeable a time reading this as I did writing it, please tell other people about the agreeable time that you had, so they can have an agreeable time too. Even if your review is only a line or two, it would be a massive help!

Amazon UK: http://amzn.to/1TXRQoP

Amazon US: http://amzn.to/1TQ5dsY

Last of all, don't be a stranger! You can get in touch, for any reason at all, by email here: nick@thawley.co.uk.

Recommended reading

For the most accessible, practical guide to mindfulness that exists (for free, no less):
Mindfulness In Plain English – Ven. Henepola Gunaratana

For a far more scientific perspective, and a great exposition of the illusion of the ego:
Waking Up – Sam Harris

For a hugely enjoyable and funny account of an ABC News anchor's sceptical foray into the world of spirituality:
10% Happier – Dan Harris

For a life-affirming look at how to best tackle adversity, inspired by Stoic philosophy:
The Obstacle Is The Way – Ryan Holiday

For the pure, concentrated insight that usually serves as the kindling for a newbie's interest in spirituality:
The Power Of Now – Eckhart Tolle

For a guide to using self-observation to figure out what to do with your life:
Be A Free Range Human – Marianne Cantwell

For a great little volume that rewards repeated reads:
Mindfulness For Cynics – Nick Thawley

Acknowledgments

I would like to thank the following locations for providing fantastic creative environments during the writing of this book:

1) Hosteria Las Islas, Isla Del Sol, Lake Titicaca, Bolivia

It's hard to complain when you're living on the island where the sun was born (look it up) and have a view over the endless, shimmering Lake Titicaca from your writing desk for £3.50 a night. However, I'm pretty sure the Bolivian ladies who ran it couldn't be bothered with me being there so long, so tried to scare me off by deliberately giving me food poisoning with a bad egg. It's not hard to complain about that.

2) Martha and Tina's Apartment, Vilcabamba, Ecuador

My biggest thanks go to Tina for hooking me up with a cheap place to stay, and to Martha for putting up with me much longer than I had initially planned. It was hard to leave an apartment situated right on the main square of tow, with £1.50 meals available in all directions, and a selection of approximately 18,000 DVD's on the shelves to practise my Spanish with in the evenings.

I'd also like to thank the following people for very generously taking the time to provide feedback on all aspects of the book:

Carlos Puyol, Olly Mitchell, Andy Greenwell, Matt Brandon, Zack Ellis, Ewan Henry, Mike Dore, Finn Kelly, Matt O Maoileoin, Hayley Davinson, Ben King, Louise Thawley, TheProf.

Honourable mentions:

> Douglas Adams' *The Hitchhiker's Guide To The Galaxy*, for pretty much exclusively influencing the writing style of this book.

> My beloved Wolfpack for repeatedly blowing my mind over the course of 3 months last year.

Appendix 1: Simple Meditation Instructions w/ Tips

Print these out, write them on post-its, tattoo them to your forehead.

1) Find a quiet (ish) room
2) Sit down, cross-legged or in a chair
3) Set a timer for 20 minutes
4) Close your eyes
5) Put all of your attention on the sensations of breathing
6) When you get distracted, return to Step 5

Top tips:

> The secret to success is consistent practice. The secret to success is consistent practice. The secret to success is consistent practice.

> Don't worry or judge yourself when you get distracted, since this is where the actual 'rep' of the exercise is done. Just gently take your attention back to your breath. *Rinse and repeat until enlightened..*

> The best time to meditate is the time you can find, but 5 minutes every day is far better than 1 hour every week. Don't skip a day just because you woke up 5 minutes later than you usually meditate – do it on the bus home if you need to.

> If you are struggling to stay focused, try counting each breath up to 5, then back down again. Once you've done this 3-4 times, give it a go without the stabilisers again.

> Remember not to covertly 'wish' that your mind would settle down, or that your knee would stop hurting, or that the timer would hurry up and go off already. Try and sit in acceptance with whatever is happening at that moment.

Appendix 2: The Five Best Ways To Practise Mindfulness

Write these out, copy them to your smartphone, tattoo them to your chest.

1) Meditation: 20 minutes on your bedroom floor in the morning is one of the most deeply beneficial daily habits I can think of. Practise consistently and you *will* notice the difference.

2) On the way to work: notice the hum of the engine, the non-existent hum of conversation between your fellow train passengers, and the hum of the slightly odd man on your left who you suspect *still* hasn't stopped humming on the train since the last time you saw him.

3) 'Mini-pauses' in your day: waiting for your computer to boot up, queueing at the bank, waiting for half of your sandwich to toast. Put your attention all the sensations you can sense – you've got nothing better to do, after all.

4) When you're in a difficult situation (job interview, public speaking, telling your parents *they're* adopted) and there's any hint of anxiety, nerves or fear: get into the present, asap – or even better, try and find five minutes directly beforehand to do so. This will ensure that your emotions

don't overwhelm you and enable you to put across the best possible version of yourself.

5) When you're enjoying a particularly delicious meal: forget everything else, and just eat. In case you need reminding: be aware of your sensations, internal narration, mastication duration, and saliva creation with a patient mindful meditation that'll provide inflation to your appreciation of the starvation termination situation.

References

[i] Fraher et al. (2016): "Mindfulness in Action: Discovering How U.S. Navy SEALs Build Capacity for Mindfulness in High-Reliability Organizations (HROs)"

[ii] The Economist (Nov 16th 2013): "The Mindfulness Business"

[iii] Tes.co.uk (Mar 12th 2014): "'Mindfulness' courses for pupils being considered by government, minister reveals"

[iv] Slagter et al. (2007): "Mental Training Affects Distribution of Limited Brain Resources"

[v] Goyal et al. (2014): "Meditation Programs for Psychological Stress and Well-being"

[vi] Hölzel et al. (2011): "Mindfulness practice leads to increases in regional brain gray matter density"

[vii] Turakitwanakan et al. (2013): "Effects of mindfulness meditation on serum cortisol of medical students."

[viii] Brickman, Coates, Janoff-Bulman (1978). "Lottery winners and accident victims: Is happiness relative?"

[ix] Jha et al. (2007): "Mindfulness training modifies subsystems of attention.", Walsh & Shapiro (2006): The meeting of meditative disciplines and western psychology: A

mutually enriching dialogue", Ren et al. (2011): "Meditation promotes insightful problem-solving by keeping people in a mindful and alert conscious state."

23179585R00086

Printed in Great Britain
by Amazon